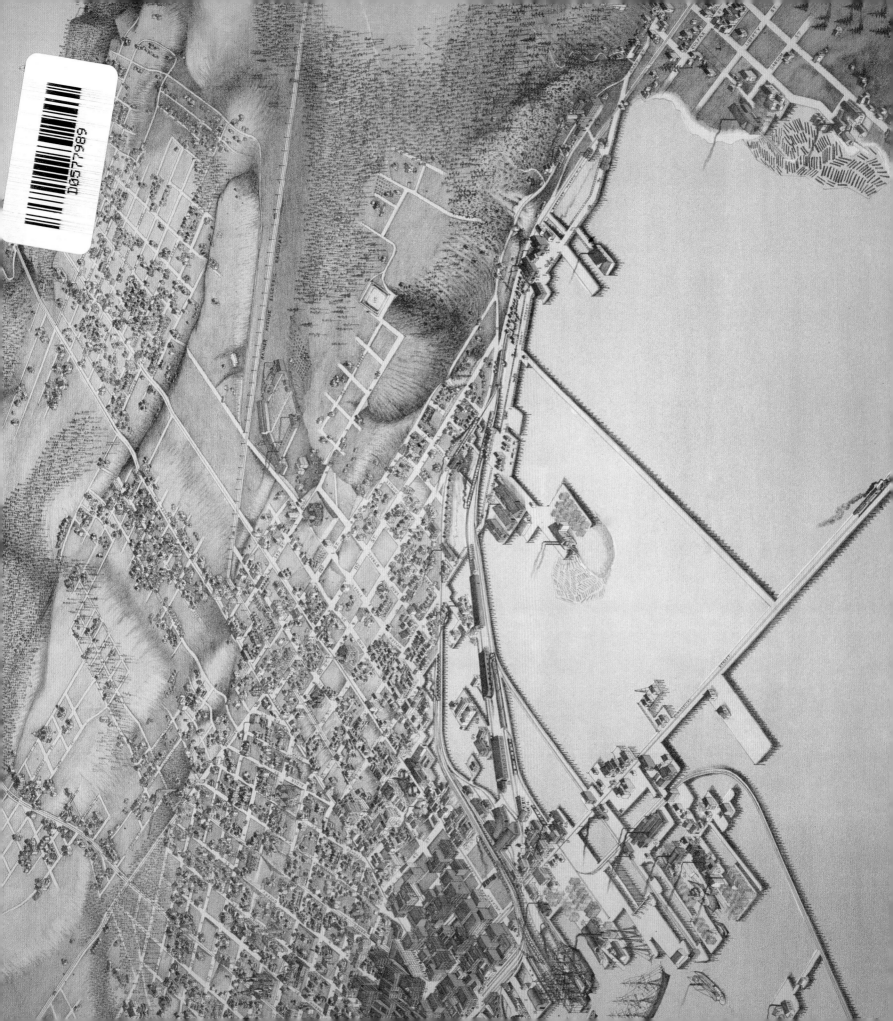

D0577989

Seattle
THEN AND NOW

Seattle

THEN AND NOW

Benjamin Lukoff

THUNDER BAY
P · R · E · S · S

San Diego, California

Thunder Bay Press

An imprint of the Baker & Taylor Publishing Group
10350 Barnes Canyon Road, San Diego, CA 92121
www.thunderbaybooks.com

Produced by Salamander Books,
an imprint of Anova Books Ltd.
10 Southcombe Street, London W14 0RA, UK

"Then and Now" is a registered trademark of Anova Books Ltd.

© 2010 Salamander Books

Copyright under International, Pan American, and Universal Copyright Conventions. All rights reserved. No part of this book may be reproduced or transmitted in any form or by any means, electronic or mechanical, including photocopying, recording, or by any information storage-and-retrieval system, without written permission from the copyright holder. Brief passages (not to exceed 1,000 words) may be quoted for reviews.

"Thunder Bay" is a registered trademark of Baker & Taylor. All rights reserved.

All notations of errors or omissions should be addressed to Thunder Bay Press, Editorial Department, at the above address. All other correspondence (author inquiries, permissions) concerning the content of this book should be addressed to Salamander Books, 10 Southcombe Street, London W14 0RA, UK.

ISBN-13: 978-1-60710-131-4
ISBN-10: 1-60710-131-9

Library of Congress Cataloging-in-Publication Data available upon request.

1 2 3 4 5 14 13 12 11 10

Printed in China

AUTHOR ACKNOWLEDGMENTS

I would like to thank my wife, Jennifer Ross, for her love and support, and my late parents, Drs. Fred and Young-Soon Lukoff, for my lifetime love of language, the arts, and learning. Thanks, Dad, for taking me "exploring" in Seattle when I was a kid.

PICTURE CREDITS

The publisher wishes to thank the following for kindly supplying the photographs that appear in this book:

"Then" photographs:
All "Then" images in the book were supplied courtesy of the Museum of History and Industry, Seattle, except for the following: Corbis: 10 inset, 14, 16, 18, 24, 26, 28, 36, 44, 106, 108 inset. Library of Congress: 6 (4a06343), 8 (3c05755). Rainier Valley Historical Society: 110. Seattle Municipal Archives: 10 main, 66 main and inset, 72, 92, 118, 142. University of Washington Libraries, Special Collections: 20, 22, 68, 74, 80, 84, 90, 108 main, 112, 124, 134, 138.

"Now" photographs:
All "Now" images were taken by Karl Mondon, except for the following: Benjamin Lukoff: 135 inset.

Pages 1 and 2 show the view from Beacon Hill, then (Museum of History and Industry) and now (Karl Mondon).

Endpapers show a map of Seattle from 1891 (Corbis).

Anova Books is committed to respecting the intellectual property rights of others. We have therefore taken all reasonable efforts to ensure that the reproduction of all content on these pages is done with the full consent of copyright owners. If you are aware of any unintentional omissions, please contact the company directly so that any necessary corrections may be made for future editions.

Introduction

Seattle is a young city. It was not until November 13, 1851, that the schooner *Exact* landed at Alki Point on Puget Sound, bringing the seven-month-long journey of the Denny party to an end. This group, led by Arthur A. Denny of Cherry Grove, Illinois, wintered on the peninsula, then scouted for more promising sites. They settled on Piner's Point, a sand spit jutting into Elliott Bay and surrounded by steep, forested hills.

The shores of Elliott Bay were already occupied by the Duwamish tribe, who had been living on the shores of Whulge—"salt water"—for many millennia. In 1792 their chief, Si'ahl, had reputedly met the naval expedition led by Captain George Vancouver, the first Europeans to explore the inland waters. In 1851 Si'ahl would greet the new settlers. Their village, initially called Duwamps after the native inhabitants, was soon named Seattle in his honor.

In the beginning, Seattle's economy largely rested on its bountiful natural resources, especially timber, which fueled the early decades of the settlement's growth. Henry Yesler's mill and others like it provided building material not only for the expanding town but for cities such as San Francisco—at that time, the largest on the West Coast. His adjacent cookhouse soon became the locus of civic activity.

Yet by 1861, when the Territorial University of Washington was established, Seattle's population numbered only 300. The head count was just over 1,000 when the city was incorporated eight years later. In 1873 Seattle was passed over for Tacoma as the western terminus of the Northern Pacific Railroad. It seemed the "Queen City," as Seattle was then known, might be eclipsed by the "City of Destiny" to the south.

However, by the late 1880s, Seattle boasted a population of over 20,000, spurred by the development of mining and transoceanic shipping, and the arrival of waves of immigrants. On June 6, 1889, a fire destroyed most of Seattle's downtown along with its docks and railroad stations. Yet, showing a characteristic resilience, the city rebuilt itself quickly, and its population soon topped 40,000. Seattle became the western terminus of the Great Northern Railway in 1893. This and the Klondike gold rush, which began in 1897, cemented Seattle's place as the Pacific Northwest's premier port city; its population doubled from 1890 to 1900, and then tripled from 1900 to 1910.

In less than a human life span, Seattle had gone from pioneer settlement to regional metropolis. The ensuing decades would make it a player on the national and world stage. William E. Boeing made Seattle an early center of aviation, both military and commercial. His firm's contribution to the success of the United States during World War II is incalculable, and during that period Seattle was a major hub of military activity. In addition to Boeing, the twentieth century also saw the local founding of UPS, PACCAR, Todd Pacific Shipyards, Nordstrom, and Eddie Bauer. The University of Washington grew into a major research institution.

Seattle was also a hotbed of social change. Though its history was far from perfect—the Native American population had long ago been dispersed, an anti-Chinese riot took place in 1886, and racial discrimination existed in housing until the 1960s—it was nevertheless the site of the country's first general strike (1919) and first racially integrated public housing project (Yesler Terrace, 1940). Seattleites also founded such early consumers' cooperatives as REI, Group Health, PCC Natural Markets, and the People's Memorial Association.

Perhaps even more striking was Seattle's topographical change. The 240-foot Denny Hill, which once stood north of downtown, was literally washed into Elliott Bay to fill the tidelands west of Beacon Hill in the early twentieth century. This resulted in the creation of Harbor Island, at the time the world's largest artificial island, at the mouth of the Duwamish River, the upper reaches of which had been straightened and channeled beyond recognition. Floating bridges, including one that is still the world's longest, were laid across Lake Washington. The lake itself was lowered by nine feet in 1916, when a ship canal was built to connect it to Puget Sound. Seattle had to expand, and it would not let its natural environment get in the way.

During the 1960s, the promise of the 1962 Century 21 Exposition that brought Seattle its Space Needle seemed to be fulfilled. Over half a million people now lived within the city limits, and its industrial future seemed secure. Though the 1971 cancellation of Boeing's supersonic transport project sent the city into an economic tailspin known as the "Boeing Bust"—which caused two real estate agents to erect a billboard near the airport that read "Will the last person leaving Seattle turn out the lights?"—the city would again recover.

Seattleites Bill Gates and Paul Allen founded Microsoft in 1975, and moved the company back to the area in 1978. It is today the cornerstone of the Puget Sound high-tech industry; this cluster includes Amazon, RealNetworks, Expedia, Nintendo of America, and Cray. Starbucks and Costco are also headquartered here, and the region has become a hub of biomedical research, which seems to be the next major growth area. As it has been throughout its history, Seattle is just as able to adapt to changing circumstances.

Despite all the changes mentioned above—or perhaps because they came so quickly—people ask if Seattle really has a history, being that the city is so young. Local journalist Knute Berger has referred to this as Seattle's "civic dementia," and attributes it to the city's frontier traditions of boosterism and transience, as well as an ever-increasing percentage of the population born somewhere else. Many other cities have had their current shape since before the *Exact* landed at Alki—comparatively speaking, Seattle has sprung up overnight. Perhaps no other American city has undergone as much transformation in as little time.

But a history it plainly does have. It began with the arrival of the Duwamish as many as 9,000 years ago, and traces of the past are visible everywhere. From the postfire buildings of Pioneer Square that were built in nonflammable brick, to the University of Washington, whose campus layout was transformed by the 1909 Alaska-Yukon-Pacific Exposition, to the city's new streetcars, some of them running on routes laid down more than a century ago, Seattle's history is there for the taking—if one only knows where to look.

CENTRAL WATERFRONT

Still a hub of activity a century later

This shot of Seattle's waterfront, part of a panorama taken by William Henry Jackson sometime between 1901 and 1906, centers on the foot of Main Street, just west of Pioneer Square. At the time, it was much the working waterfront, with piers jutting into Elliott Bay as far north as Smith Cove, and Railroad Avenue and the lines of the Northern Pacific and Great Northern paralleling the shore. In the foreground are the Ocean and City docks, built in 1901 by the Pacific Coast Company. The City Dock is

occupied by Lilly, Bogardus, and Company, a seed, hay, and grain concern. Next to it is docked the *Alice Gertrude*, part of the Puget Sound Navigation Company's Mosquito Fleet. The tops of the Puget Sound Machinery Depot (1890), Schwabacher Hardware Company (1892), Mutual Life Building (1892), Hotel Northern (1891), Grand Central Hotel (1890), and Seattle Hotel (1890) are just visible behind the piers. Atop First Hill, the 1890 King County Courthouse can be seen.

The *Alice Gertrude* was wrecked in 1907 and the City Dock was reconstructed in the 1930s. It is now slated to become part of the expansion of Colman Dock, home to Washington State Ferries, heir to the Mosquito Fleet. Many Pioneer Square buildings from the turn of the century survive—the entire neighborhood is now both a federal and local historic district—though they are more likely today to house office space and

artists' lofts. Seattle still has a working harbor, but its center of activity has shifted to the container terminals on Harbor Island and around the mouth of the Duwamish Waterway. The Central Waterfront is now home to tourist activities, including Ivar's Acres of Clams, Waterfront Park, the Seattle Aquarium, the Edgewater Hotel, the Olympic Sculpture Park, and terminals for tour boats, catamarans, and cruise ships.

SECOND AVE. & MARION ST.
Seattle Wash. July 1889
© McManus 1912

GRAHAM.
TAILOR.

R.G. CALDWELL,
DENTIST.

G. & CO.
ISTS.

DAVID SHINER'S
EMPLOYMENT OFFICE

AVE UNION FURNITURE MFG. CO.

THE FAMOUS

Dr. M. F. Shiun De.
C. RHEI

BOOKS

SECOND AND MARION

Marking the northern limit of the devastating 1889 fire

Left: This photo was taken looking northwest from the corner of Second and Marion streets in July 1889, just a month after the Great Seattle Fire that destroyed the city's sixty-four-acre commercial core on June 6. Though there were no fatalities, the fire—which started just a block away at Front and Madison—swept through nearly thirty blocks of wooden buildings and wharves. It left what Rudyard Kipling, who arrived in town shortly after, called "a horrible black smudge, as though a Hand had come down and rubbed the place smooth." Rebuilding quickly began, this time in "fireproof" stone and brick. Second Street, as it was then known, was a firebreak this far north, which explains the intact houses on its east side.

Above: After the fire, Seattle's commercial core shifted north. Second Avenue, which became the city's main thoroughfare for the better part of half a century, has been called the city's architectural "Canyon of Dreams" by local historian Paul Dorpat. The Burke Building was erected on the northwest corner of Second and Marion in 1891 and stood there until it was razed to make way for the thirty-seven-story Federal Building. Though preservationists failed in their quest to save the Richardsonian Romanesque structure, its entry arches were preserved and stand in front of the building to this day. In use since 1976, it was named seven years later for the late senator Henry M. Jackson. Across the street is the 1983 Wells Fargo Center, and farther north on Second stand the 1850 Federal Reserve Building and the Second and Seneca Building.

THE DENNY REGRADE

Seattle's city planners had no hesitation in removing a hill

Left: Seattle, like many other cities worldwide, is said to have been built on seven hills, even though topographically speaking this is inaccurate. Whatever number is used, it was decreased by one between 1900 and 1930, when the 240-foot-high Denny Hill was excavated into Elliott Bay in what is known as the Denny Regrade. The inset shows the former Denny Hotel, which stood atop the hill on the block between Second and Third avenues and Stewart and Virginia streets. Begun in 1890, it was completed in 1903, when it was renamed the Washington. It is shown here in 1907, just before its removal as part of the first phase. This took away the southern and western half of the hill in an effort to ease the city's expansion northward. However, the project stopped at Fifth Avenue; what was left of Denny Hill became even more of a hindrance to development than it had been. The main photo shows the necessary second phase in progress during the fall of 1929, from the intersection of Fifth Avenue and Battery Street.

Above: Since the 1962 World's Fair, Fifth Avenue south of Broad Street has been dominated by the Seattle Center Monorail. Eight million people rode the monorail during the fair, more than covering the cost of construction. The original trains have run the mile-long route between Seattle Center and Westlake Center ever since, logging their millionth mile in 2008. Annual ridership is around 1.5 million, and the system makes a yearly profit—reputedly the only public-transit system in the country to do so. In 2002 the monorail's future seemed in doubt, as the voters of Seattle approved a citywide system that would incorporate the Fifth Avenue route; nevertheless, it was made an official city landmark in 2003. Voters canceled the project in 2005. In the foreground are the grates of the Battery Street Tunnel, built in 1952 to connect the Alaskan Way Viaduct to Aurora Avenue North and allow U.S. Route 99 to bypass Belltown traffic. The cylindrical Westin Hotel (1968) can be seen in the distance.

VIEW NORTH FROM THE SMITH TOWER

Viewing Lake Union from the Smith Tower is a much tougher prospect today

Left: This photo was taken looking north from the 462-foot Smith Tower shortly after it was completed in 1914. As Seattle's tallest building, it was the only location from which a view like this could be had, encompassing the central business district and showing Queen Anne Hill, Wallingford, and Capitol Hill in the background, with almost all of Lake Union visible at center. In the foreground are the domed First Methodist Episcopal Church (1910), the Rainier Club (1904), and the Central Building (1907), which was built on the old church site. To the north can be seen Seattle's Carnegie library (1904) and Providence Hospital (1882). Queen Anne High School (1909) can just be made out atop the hill. The remnants of Denny Hill are visible in front of Queen Anne Hill. A massive regrade, whose first phase ended in 1911, removed most of the 240-foot rise into Elliott Bay.

Above: Today's skyscrapers make a northward view from Pioneer Square beyond downtown impossible. The church, now a recital hall, remains, as do the Rainier Club and Central Building, both now city landmarks. The library and hospital, however, have long since been replaced, and the high school is now condominiums. At center stands the Pacific Building office tower (1970), with the 1930 YMCA Building just visible behind it. In the background, from left to right, are the forty-seven-story Wells Fargo Center (1983), forty-story Fourth and Madison Building (2002), forty-two-story 901 Fifth Avenue Building (1973), and the twenty-eight-story Renaissance Madison Hotel (1983). Between the last two can be seen the Nakamura Courthouse (1940), built on the hospital grounds and now serving the U.S. Court of Appeals.

GASWORKS

From a gasworks to Gas Works Park, with all the apparatus of industry

Left: This photo, taken from the northeast slope of Queen Anne Hill around 1910, shows Brown's Point jutting into Lake Union, with Eastlake, the University District, and the University of Washington campus in the background. The peninsula south of Wallingford was plotted in 1883 by Judge Thomas Burke and his wife Caroline. Two years later, Burke founded the Seattle, Lake Shore, and Eastern Railway, later part of the Northern Pacific. One of its customers was the Seattle Gas Light Company's coal gasification plant, seen at center. The company, which since 1873 had been operating from Gas Cove near Chinatown, began to acquire land here in 1900; the plant opened in 1906. Just visible at center is the 1891 Latona Bridge. Originally for streetcars, it was widened eleven years later to accommodate all traffic. As the main route from downtown to the University District, it carried four million visitors to the Alaska-Yukon-Pacific Exposition on the university campus the year before this photo was taken.

Above: In 1937 the plant switched from coal to oil, and in 1956 it was shut down, as natural gas became more popular. Six years later the city bought the site, and instead of demolishing the gasworks and developing the acreage, decided to turn it into a park, leaving much of the industrial apparatus intact. Designed by Richard Haag and originally named for Myrtle Edwards, the late city councilor who was instrumental in its preservation, it was renamed Gas Works Park at her family's request. Gas Works Park opened in 1975 and was made a city landmark in 2002. It is a favored spot for fireworks shows, kite flying, and picnicking. The railroad right-of-way, abandoned in 1971 by the Burlington Northern, is now the Burke-Gilman Trail, which opened in 1978 and now stretches twenty-eight miles from Ballard to Lake Sammamish. Portage Bay is now crossed by the University Bridge, built in 1919, and the Ship Canal Bridge, built for Interstate 5 in 1961. At far left are the Hotel Deca (1931) and UW Tower (1973).

FIRST HILL AND CIVIC CENTER

The spires of St. James still gaze over the city

Left: This photo, taken sometime in the early 1910s, offers a view of the eastern part of downtown, with First Hill at right, Capitol Hill and its 1907 water tower in the center distance, and Lake Union and the broad avenues of Wallingford at left. On First Hill is St. James Cathedral (1907), seat of the Catholic Diocese of Seattle. On the vacant lot bounded by Columbia and Marion streets and Fifth and Sixth avenues had stood the Rainier Hotel, built in 1889 and demolished in preparation for the regrading of Sixth. Just to its west is the dome of the First Methodist Episcopal Church, completed in 1910. On the same block is the Rainier Club building (1904). This was the fourth home of Seattle's preeminent private club, which was founded in 1888.

Above: The Rainier Club, First Methodist, and St. James have been dwarfed by their surroundings, the most prominent of which are the seventy-four-story Columbia Center (1985) and sixty-two-story Seattle Municipal Tower (1990). At bottom right is the Seattle Civic Center, which includes the green-roofed Seattle City Hall (2003) and the Seattle Justice Center (2001), housing police headquarters and the municipal court. In the 1990s, the Methodist congregation began to contemplate a move, as their building was in poor repair. A landmark nomination was blocked in 1996, and the dome's destruction seemed assured. However, in 2006, a deal was brokered whereby only the 1950s annex would be razed; First Methodist moved to Lower Queen Anne in 2007, and the old sanctuary is now the Daniels Recital Hall. The Rainier Club, which was racially integrated in 1968 and sexually integrated in 1978, remains Seattle's premier club. It was designated a national landmark in 1976 and a city landmark in 1987.

HOOVERVILLE DOCKS

Waiting for the tide of the Great Depression to turn

This photograph, taken in April 1941, shows Seattle's Hooverville on Elliott Bay, "one of the largest and longest-lasting" in the country according to the Great Depression in Washington State Project. At its peak, it had 1,200 inhabitants on nine acres of land at the foot of Atlantic Street, formerly the site of a shipyard. During World War I, Skinner and Eddy produced thirty-two ships for the government's Emergency Fleet Corporation—a national record—yet the postwar depression caused the yard to close in 1920. The Pacific Steamship Company moved in, but their grand redevelopment plan failed to come to fruition. The subsequent Depression hit Seattle hard, as much of its economy depended on shipping. The first squatters began moving to the property in 1931. In 1940 the U.S. Army purchased the tract for a supply depot, and a month before this photo was taken, evictions began. The Puget Sound Navigation Company's ferry *Kalakala* is in the background, on its way to Seattle's Colman Dock from Bremerton.

Demolition of Hooverville began in the spring of 1941 and by November of that year the million-square-foot Seattle Army Depot stood on the site. A month after Pearl Harbor, it became the Seattle Port of Embarkation, one of the country's largest. By 1944 the army had commissioned three new piers. The Seattle Army Terminal, as it was renamed in 1955, operated until 1958, and the site was acquired by the city in 1964. The U.S. Coast Guard has leased Pier 36 since 1973, and occupies the old Pacific Steamship Company building. The old depot is now a federal warehouse, and the rest of the land is a massive container terminal. The view to the north is dominated by Seattle's postwar skyline, as well as a single-track remnant of the once-mighty Railroad Avenue. The 1953 Alaskan Way Viaduct (right) carries Washington State Route 99 along the waterfront. It was damaged in the 2001 Nisqually earthquake but still serves traffic.

AYPE AND RAINIER VISTA

The University of Washington's layout was based on that of the World's Fair

Left: The Alaska-Yukon-Pacific Exposition (AYPE) took place in Seattle from June 1 to October 16, 1909. It drew almost four million visitors to the campus of the University of Washington, which had moved to the forested tract fourteen years earlier. The famed Olmsted brothers, who also designed many of Seattle's parks and parkways, were engaged to plan the grounds, and oriented them on an axis pointing at Mount Rainier, just over fifty miles to the southeast. This world's fair, which was originally planned for 1907, the tenth anniversary of the Klondike gold rush, soon saw its scope expand to cover the rest of the Pacific Northwest, and indeed the Pacific Rim. This photograph was taken from the top of the United States Government Building. On the left are the Hawaiian, Mines, and Manufacturing buildings; on the right are those of Alaska, Fisheries, and Agriculture. Cascade Court is in the center, in front of the Arctic Circle and Geyser Basin. Beyond the pool is Rainier Vista and the 14,411-foot mountain itself.

Above: After the AYPE closed, the Olmsteds drew up another plan for the campus, retaining much of the fair's layout. This 1914 plan, which called for the uniform adoption of collegiate Gothic, in contrast to the random architectural styles then in place, was revised by Carl F. Gould and Charles H. Bebb in 1915, and implemented by their firm over the next twenty-four years. At left is their Suzzallo Library (1926, with additions in 1935, 1963, and 1990), the centerpiece of campus; to the right is the administration building, Gerberding Hall (1949). The Geyser Basin, known informally as Frosh Pond, remains in place. It is now adorned with Drumheller Fountain, a gift to the university on its 1961 centennial. In the foreground is Central Plaza. Originally an expanse of grass, it was paved over in 1969 during the construction of an underground garage, and almost immediately nicknamed Red Square. It is unclear whether this refers to the one in Moscow or simply to the color of the bricks. Mount Rainier is obscured by low clouds in the main image; the inset shows the vista on a clear day.

UNIVERSITY OF WASHINGTON QUAD

A prime example of collegiate Gothic style

Left: This photograph, taken sometime in the early 1930s, shows the southwestern end of the Liberal Arts Quadrangle on the campus of the University of Washington. Laid out in the collegiate Gothic style by campus architects Carl F. Gould and Charles H. Bebb in 1915, it is here seen framed by Philosophy Hall (1920), at right, and Condon Hall (1932), home to the law school, at left. In between the two is the university's library, built in 1926 and named in 1933 for Henry Suzzallo, the university's president from 1915 to 1926. Not seen are Home Economics and Education halls, built in 1916 and 1922, respectively, nor the open northeast end of the expanse. The clear sky is mirrored in the featureless lawn, as yet unmarked by trees or other vegetation, and a clear view of Capitol Hill can be had between Philosophy Hall and the library.

Above: Today's Quad, as it is commonly known, remains the heart of the university. Philosophy Hall was renamed after the late professor William Savery in 1947, Education after regent Winlock Miller in 1954, and Home Economics after the late professor Effie Raitt in 1946. Condon—still visible here, though largely covered by trees—was renamed after the late professor Herbert Gowen in 1977. It is now home to the Department of Asian Languages and Literature and the East Asia Library, which grew out of the Department of Oriental Subjects, founded by Gowen in 1909. Later buildings not visible here include Smith Hall (1940) and the Art and Music buildings (1949 and 1950). The Quad lawn is now lined with Yoshino cherry trees, moved here from Montlake in 1964 to save them from the path of freeway construction. Already decades old at the time, they are nearing the end of their natural lives, and are being systematically replaced in a project that began in 1999.

ELLIOTT BAY / INDUSTRIAL DISTRICT

Barely recognizable today, a century after being filled

Above: This photo was taken around 1882, looking south from the vicinity of Pine Street. It shows a Seattle that had turned thirty the year before, and possessed just over 3,500 residents. Most of what we see in the foreground are houses and small farms, with marine, commercial, and industrial activity concentrated in Pioneer Square, at center. In December of this year, the first steamship left Seattle for Asia—the *Madras*, on its way to Honolulu and Hong Kong—after having brought with it over 600 Chinese, mostly laborers. The Elliott Bay mudflats stretch clear to the foot of Beacon Hill; they are crossed by the trestle of the Columbia and Puget Sound Railroad, bound for Georgetown and beyond. The mouth of the Duwamish River and the ridge of West Seattle are visible in the distance.

Right: In a series of fills, the mudflats were covered during the early decades of the twentieth century. Elliott Bay was pushed back to the mouth of the river, which was itself straightened and channeled into the Duwamish Waterway. In 1909 Harbor Island was built between the new Industrial District and West Seattle. It was the largest artificial island in the world at the time, a title it held until 1938. It now encompasses nearly 400 acres and is the center of Seattle's container port. The Port of Seattle, which was founded in 1911, is now the tenth busiest port in North America; if combined with Tacoma, it would be fourth. Qwest Field (2002), home to the National Football League's Seahawks and Major League Soccer's Sounders, and Safeco Field (1999), home to Major League Baseball's Mariners, sit at the district's north end. The old shoreline is still evident in the placement of multistory buildings, which are rare south of Pioneer Square because of the risk of soil liquefaction during earthquakes.

FRONT STREET / FIRST AVENUE

Looking south toward Pioneer Square

This photograph was taken looking south from the intersection of Front and Madison streets. Pioneer and historian Thomas Prosch has the date as 1880, while modern historian Paul Dorpat places it as 1878 or 1879. The foreground figures are Andrew W. Piper, his son Wallis, and their dog. Piper, who was originally from Germany, operated the Puget Sound Candy Factory, a confectioner's shop and bakery on Front Street, in addition to being an amateur painter. Prosch would rhapsodize about his cream cakes in Piper's 1904 obituary. Shown here at far right is part of the Pontius Building. Farther south is John A. Woodward's flour mill, then the North Pacific Brewery—descendant of one of the city's first, established in 1865. Behind those, the third story of Pioneer Square's Arlington Hotel is visible. Elliott Bay can be seen between the Pontius and Woodward properties as well as in the distance, washing up against the foot of Beacon Hill.

Front Street is now First Avenue, and the bay has been pushed behind a seawall two blocks to the west. Most of the structures in the historical photo perished in Seattle's Great Fire of June 6, 1889, which started on this corner in the Pontius Building. Today, that corner is occupied by the Art Deco–style Federal Office Building, built in 1933 and added to the National Register of Historic Places in 1979. In 1974 it was supplemented by a thirty-seven-story skyscraper across the street. This tower was named the Henry M. Jackson Federal Building in 1983 after the long-serving U.S. senator died unexpectedly. Farther down First are the Exchange Building (1930) and the postfire Colman Building (1889, with multiple subsequent additions). The Pipers, meanwhile, are today best known for Piper's Canyon, their homestead in the north end of the city along Puget Sound. This became Carkeek Park in 1929. Their name lives on in Piper's Creek, to which salmon have begun to return, and Piper's Orchard, a remnant of Wilhelmina Piper's apple grove.

WESTLAKE BOULEVARD / WESTLAKE CENTER

Westlake Park is now Seattle's main gathering place

Left: This photo, taken circa 1909, shows the recently created intersection of what was then Westlake Boulevard and Fourth Avenue, with the flatiron Plaza Hotel at center and the zeitgeist-capturing Radium Hotel at left. As it was taken between regrades of Denny Hill, Fourth Avenue still shows a steep slope, though Westlake—the southern portion of which was laid out in 1906—provides a straight shot to the southern shores of Lake Union and beyond. Promotional material for the 1909 Alaska–Yukon–Pacific Exposition taking place at the University of Washington campus notes that "13 different [street]car lines pass directly in front of the Plaza." Indeed, at least three can be seen here. Just visible up Fourth Avenue from the hotel is Carpenters Hall, which housed Local 131 of the United Brotherhood of Carpenters and Joiners of America. It was regarded as one of the most powerful unions in the city.

Above: This portion of the Denny Regrade was finished by 1911, producing the flat topography that now characterizes the neighborhood. In 1962 the intersection became the south terminus of the monorail constructed for the Century 21 Exposition. At the same time, plans for the area's redevelopment were floated. However, it was not until 1986 that this portion of Westlake Avenue was vacated in preparation for the construction of Westlake Center, which opened in 1988. A combination shopping mall and office tower, it stands 330 feet above what is now Westlake Park—Seattle's informal town square and the site of many rallies and protests. The Seattle Center Monorail now stops a block north, at Fifth and Westlake, and the new Seattle Streetcar to South Lake Union ends just north of that. Underground is the Westlake station of the Downtown Seattle Transit Tunnel, which serves as the northern terminus of the new Central Link light-rail line.

29

SEATTLE–TACOMA INTERNATIONAL AIRPORT

Tacoma influenced the siting of the airport with a $100,000 lure

Left: Boeing Field had served as Seattle's primary passenger airport since 1928, but was soon considered for replacement because of the hazard to navigation posed by its location against Beacon Hill. When World War II began, the federal government took control of the airport, and civilian traffic moved to Paine Field in Snohomish County. Meanwhile, the Civil Aviation Authority put up $1 million toward the construction of a new, larger facility for the region. After Tacoma promised an additional $100,000 if the new airport were situated closer to Pierce County than a proposed location on Lake Sammamish, the Port of Seattle selected a 907-acre tract near Bow Lake, and construction began in 1943. Seattle-Tacoma Airport, often referred to as "Sea-Tac," opened on October 31, 1944, and scheduled commercial flights began on September 1, 1947. The modern main terminal building was dedicated on July 9, 1949, on which day Sea-Tac added "International" to its name. It is shown here during a military air show, part of the opening-day festivities.

Above: This is the runway side of Sea-Tac's main terminal, with two Alaska Airlines planes in front of Concourse C, one of its four wings. Alaska Airlines, founded in that state in 1932, is now headquartered just south of Sea-Tac, which serves as its hub. The old control tower, damaged in the 2001 Nisqually earthquake, now directs ramp, as opposed to runway, traffic. Sea-Tac has expanded considerably since the 1950s. A second runway was built in the early 1970s, and a third, after much controversy, opened in late 2008. The main terminal itself was first expanded in the 1970s and underwent renovation in 2005. In 1983 Sea-Tac was renamed after the late senator Henry M. Jackson, but the Port of Seattle reversed itself early the next year after protests from Tacoma. Sea-Tac was the seventeenth-busiest airport in the United States in 2009, handling just over 31.2 million passengers.

KING COUNTY COURTHOUSE

Officially, it stood on First Hill; unofficially, it stood atop Profanity Hill

Left: In 1890, having outgrown an 1876 building that was sold to the City of Seattle to serve as its city hall, King County moved its operations to the top of First Hill at Seventh Avenue and Alder Street. The $200,000 building was designed by twenty-six-year-old Willis A. Ritchie, who went on to design courthouses for Whatcom, Jefferson, Thurston, Clark, and Spokane counties. Its location on the commanding heights of First Hill, surrounded by the mansions of successful businessmen, pioneer families, and other grandees, was at first thought to be a boon. However, Seventh and Alder happened to be where First Hill had one of its steepest grades. This supposedly made those who had to scale its heights curse its location, hence the nickname "Profanity Hill."

Above: The undated archival photograph was taken sometime between 1903 and 1909, when it appeared in a program for the Alaska-Yukon-Pacific Exposition. In 1916 the county government moved back down the hill. The old courthouse stood until 1931. Interstate 5, built through First Hill and downtown in the early 1960s, now covers the site of the old courthouse. On either side of Jefferson Street, which now dead-ends at Sixth Avenue, are the King County Jail, which opened in 1986, and the county's 2005 parking garage, featuring Michael Spafford's *Falling Figures: Five Stages*.

BOEING RED BARN

Dating back to a time when Boeing made its name manufacturing seaplanes

Left: In 1910 William Boeing paid Edward W. Heath $10 for his bankrupt shipyard on the western bank of the Duwamish River, where the aviation pioneer's yacht was under construction. The purchase included the Red Barn, built the year before and shown here in June 1917. Boeing would also manufacture seaplane floats at the facility; main production took place at his boathouse at the foot of Roanoke Street on Lake Union. In 1916, following the successful maiden flight of his seaplane, the *Bluebill*, he incorporated the Pacific Aero Products Company. Boeing moved production to the Duwamish after the U.S. Navy ordered fifty of its Model C seaplanes to serve as training aircraft for World War I, which the United States had entered in April 1917. Three weeks after the declaration of war, Pacific Aero Products was renamed the Boeing Airplane Company, a name it would carry for the next forty-four years.

Above: The Boeing Company, which adopted its shorter name in 1961, merged with McDonnell Douglas in 1997, and moved its corporate headquarters to Chicago in 2001. It is still best known for its commercial airplanes division, headquartered in the Seattle suburb of Renton, and its military division, the third-largest defense contractor in the world. It has also diversified into satellites, rockets, and computers. Though Seattle has likewise diversified beyond aircraft, Boeing is still the state's largest private employer. The Red Barn remained on the Duwamish River until 1975. That year, the Port of Seattle, which by then owned the site, donated it to the Museum of Flight. It was floated down the river and installed next to the county airport, Boeing Field. Three years later, it was added to the National Register of Historic Places. The Museum of Flight, which opened in 1968 at the Seattle Center, moved into the Red Barn in 1983, and opened the attached Great Gallery in 1987.

UNION STATION

Once the "handsomest" station on the Union Pacific Railroad

Left: The Union Pacific Railroad (UPRR) began construction on the Oregon and Washington Station in January 1910. Designed by Daniel J. Patterson, who also worked on a number of stations for the Southern Pacific, it was named for the Oregon and Washington Railroad, the local subsidiary of the UPRR. The Beaux Arts building at the corner of South Jackson Street and Fourth Avenue South opened on May 20, 1911. As it also served the Milwaukee Road, it came to be known as Union Station. Union Pacific president Robert S. Lovett called it "the handsomest on Harriman's lines," a reference to E. H. Harriman, UPRR president from 1903 to his death in 1909. In the foreground of this 1911 photo are the shared tracks of the Great Northern and Northern Pacific railways, as well as one of Seattle's then-ubiquitous streetcars. Chinatown and the newly built Alps Hotel are visible in the distance.

Above: Union Station served the Milwaukee Road until 1961, when it discontinued the Olympian Hiawatha. Union Pacific ceased all passenger operations on May 1, 1971, the day Amtrak was founded; subsequent passenger rail service out of Seattle was from the adjacent King Street Station only. Union Station, which was placed on the National Register of Historic Places in 1974, stood vacant for many years. In the late 1990s, the developers Nitze-Stagen and Microsoft cofounder Paul Allen's investment vehicle, Vulcan Inc., purchased the station and rail yards from the UPRR, and began renovation and construction. The 505 and 605 Union Station buildings can be seen behind the original structure; the latter for many years housed the offices of Amazon.com. The station itself had originally been considered as a central transit hub for Seattle's new bus tunnel and light-rail line. In 1999 it was sold to Sound Transit, the regional transportation authority, and now serves as its headquarters. The grand departure hall is often rented out for events.

FERRY KALAKALA / CENTRAL WATERFRONT

The cross-Sound bridges have failed to materialize, so the ferries continue to run

Left: In 1935 the *Kalakala* had just been rebuilt from the hulk of the San Francisco ferry *Peralta*. Billed as the world's first streamlined vessel, with an aerodynamic steel-and-copper superstructure overlaid with aluminum paint, the Art Deco ferry boasted what was then the largest-ever engine in a ship of its kind. It made six round-trips daily between Seattle and Bremerton for the Puget Sound Navigation Company (PSNC), whose Seattle terminal, at the foot of Marion Street, was Colman Dock. Rebuilt after the Great Fire of 1889, the terminal was adorned with a dome and tower in 1908, which were themselves rebuilt after a collision in 1912. To the south were Piers 1 and 2, constructed by the Northern Pacific Railway between 1901 and 1904. Pier 1, home to the city's port warden and harbormaster, occupied the site of Puget Sound's first steam-powered sawmill, built by Henry Yesler in 1852. From north to south, the St. James Cathedral (1907), the Exchange Building (1930), Harborview Hospital (1931), and the Smith Tower (1914) are prominent above the ridge of First Hill.

Above: The PSNC—popularly known as the Black Ball Line—continued to run ferries on Puget Sound until 1951, when it shut down those routes over a fare dispute with the government. The state took over the lines on June 1 of that year, anticipating that cross-Sound bridges and tunnels would soon be built. These never materialized, and Washington State Ferries' fleet is today the largest in the country and third-largest in the world. Annual ridership is twenty-three million, carried on twenty-three vessels from twenty terminals, including one on Vancouver Island north of Victoria, British Columbia. Victoria is also the northern end of the Black Ball's sole remaining route, across the Strait of Juan de Fuca from Port Angeles. Ferries still depart from Colman Dock, which was completely rebuilt in 1961. Many of the buildings extant in the 1930s remain, though they are no longer as prominent. There have been calls to remove the 1953 Alaskan Way Viaduct and reconnect the waterfront to the city's commercial core. The *Kalakala* stopped running in 1967 and is now awaiting restoration in Tacoma.

PIKE PLACE MARKET

Seattleites have been meeting the producer since 1907

Left: Before 1907, Seattle-area farmers sold most of their goods to the middlemen of Produce Row, located northwest of Pioneer Square. That year, the city authorized a market at the newly planked Pike Place, on a bluff above Elliott Bay, where the public could "Meet the Producer." It opened on August 17, and Frank Goodwin, who owned the Leland Hotel (far left) as well as the land along Pike Place, had the Main Arcade built by winter. The Sanitary Public Market (far right) was built three years later, and the Corner Market, named for its location at the intersection of First Avenue and Pike Street, came in 1912. Topped in this shot by billboards erected by local advertising pioneers Foster and Kleiser, it also carries placards for the city's largest real-estate firm, Henry Broderick Inc., just above the signs for Three Girls Bread, the Corner Market's first business. At far left is part of the sign for Bartell Drugs' store No. 3. Goodwin took over that building in 1916 and renamed it the Economy Market.

Above: In the 1950s, a parking garage was proposed for the site; in the 1960s, the specter of its redevelopment as the Pike Plaza office and housing complex galvanized a preservation movement led by architect Victor Steinbrueck. His name now graces a park at the market's northern end. In 1970 a federal historic district was created, and in 1971 Seattleites approved a larger city one. In 1973 the Market Preservation and Development Authority was created. It now owns or manages most of the buildings in the district. Pike Place Market—by some accounts the oldest continually operating farmer's market in the country—has changed a great deal over the years. There are no commercial farms left within the city limits, and the market's vendors are more likely to be Hmong than Japanese, who made up the vast majority of stallholders in the decades preceding World War II. Yet it remains one of the best places in town to—as the sign above the Leland Hotel invites—"Meet the Producer" of fruits, vegetables, flowers, seafood, and crafts.

SMITH TOWER / KING COUNTY COURTHOUSE

Seattle's landmark tower is still one of the tallest buildings in the city

Left: This photo, taken in 1921, shows, from left to right, the Smith Tower (1914), Arctic Club Building/Hotel Seward (1909), and County-City Building (1916). City Hall Park (improved in 1911 as Dilling Park, named after the mayor at the time) is in the foreground at the intersection of Fourth Avenue and Dilling Way. The Smith Tower, built by Lyman C. Smith of Smith-Corona typewriter fame, was Seattle's first skyscraper. At 462 feet, it was the tallest building west of Ohio. The Arctic Club was a social club for gold rush veterans founded in 1908 and which moved into a new building two blocks north in 1916. The County-City Building was erected on the site of the Yesler Mansion, last home of pioneer Henry L. Yesler, which burned down in 1901. The park occupied the site of King County's first courthouse (1876–90), later Seattle's city hall (1890–1909).

Above: In 1931 nine stories were added to the County-City Building, the top three of which made up the King County Jail. (The jail is now housed two blocks east; a skybridge for prisoner transport now connects the two over the King County Administration Building.) In 1962 a new city hall was built, and the 1916 building became known as the King County Courthouse. Five years later, the building was remodeled; many of these changes have been subsequently reversed. The courthouse was designated a county landmark in 1987. The Arctic Club Building, now known as the Morrison Hotel, has long served as supportive housing and a homeless shelter. The Smith Tower, which was designated a city landmark in 1987, is still the seventeenth-tallest building in the city. It has twice undergone renovation and was a popular office location during the dot-com boom.

PIONEER SQUARE AND PERGOLA

Much has changed, but the 1909 iron-and-glass pergola remains

Left: This photo, taken around 1910 at the intersection of First Avenue, James Street, and Yesler Way, shows passengers boarding a streetcar of the Yesler and James Street Cable Car Company. This ran to Leschi Park on Lake Washington. The iron-and-glass pergola, designed by Julian Everett, was built the year before as a streetcar stop and entrance to an elaborate underground comfort station. To the south is the Seattle Hotel (1890), the last of three to be built on the triangular block created by the clash of Arthur Denny's and David S. "Doc" Maynard's street grids. Behind the pergola stand the Pioneer (1892) and Howard (1890) buildings, designed by Elmer Fisher, and the Lowman and Hanford (1892) and Lowman (1906) buildings, designed by Emil DeNeuf. The Pioneer Building, begun by early settler Henry Yesler and completed in the year of his death, was named "the finest building west of Chicago" by the American Institute of Architects. All were early examples of rebuilding with nonflammable bricks from the "burnt district" left behind by the Great Fire of 1889.

Above: The streetcars have gone, as has the Seattle Hotel, demolished in 1961 and replaced with a parking garage. However, the rest of Pioneer Square remains largely intact, thanks to the creation of a historical district in 1970 and benign neglect for many years after. Though the restrooms were closed in the 1940s, the pergola remained standing for decades, undergoing restoration in the early 1970s and being placed on the National Register of Historic Places in 1977. However, it was destroyed by a wayward semi truck in early 2001. Rebuilding began immediately, using much of the original material, and with archival documents as guidance—the original plans had been lost. The new pergola reopened nineteen months after the accident. Pioneer Square is also the centerpiece of the Underground Tour, which leaves from and ends at the Pioneer Building. The tour, which began in 1965, offers an opportunity for the public to walk the subterranean passageways that were created when the entire neighborhood was raised twelve to thirty feet after the Great Fire.

PIONEER SQUARE TOTEM POLE

Brazenly stolen from the Tlingit, later destroyed by arson

This photo of Pioneer Place Park can have been taken no earlier than 1909, considering the presence of the Iron Pergola. It features a totem pole erected in 1899 by the Seattle Chamber of Commerce. This was not specially commissioned, however, but stolen—by fifteen members of the chamber, including its president—from a Tlingit village on Tongass Island, Alaska. They had been visiting as part of a "goodwill tour" sponsored by the *Seattle Post-Intelligencer* newspaper. Eight were later indicted by a grand jury for theft—of government, rather than Tlingit, property—but the charges were later dropped. The Tlingits nevertheless pressed a claim of $20,000, and settled for $500 in compensation for the 110-year-old pole. Behind the pergola is the Sanderson Block (1890), whose architect, W. E. Boone, is said to have been a direct descendant of Daniel Boone. An advertisement for Olympia Beer, brewed near the state capital sixty miles to the southwest, sits atop the building.

A pole still stands in Pioneer Square, but it is a replica. The original pole was destroyed by arson in 1938 and replaced by one commissioned under the auspices of the Depression-era Civilian Conservation Corps. (The ashes of the 1790 pole were returned to Alaska.) The new pole, carved under the direction of Tlingit sculptor Charles Brown, was erected in 1940. The rest of the original buildings still stand, with the notable exception of the 1890 Seattle Hotel, which became an office building in the early decades of the twentieth century. By the early 1960s it stood vacant, and was replaced by a parking garage known as the Sinking Ship, from its uncanny resemblance to such a vessel when viewed head-on. The hotel's demolition, part of a plan to level the bulk of the Pioneer Square neighborhood, helped galvanize a preservation movement. This culminated with the entire district being placed on the National Register of Historic Places in June 1970.

CHIEF SEATTLE FOUNTAIN

Without the chief, Seattle might have been known as Duwamps

This photo, taken around 1925 in front of the Plaza Hotel at Fourth and Westlake avenues, shows one of three fountains sculpted in 1909 by James A. Wehn, Seattle's "First Sculptor." It features a bust of Si'ahl, better known as (Noah) Sealth or Chief Seattle. The "new style drinking fountains," with their large basins, were able to serve the needs of horses and dogs as well as humans. Si'ahl, born sometime in the 1780s, was leader of the Suquamish and Duwamish tribes when white settlers began to arrive on the latter's land. A signatory to the 1855 Point Elliott Treaty that ceded Native American lands to the federal government, Si'ahl was welcoming to the settlers, and his tribes did not participate in the 1856 Battle of Seattle. The white settlement on Elliott Bay was originally called Duwamps—however, when the first plots were filed in 1853, they were for the Town of Seattle, at the instigation of David S. "Doc" Maynard, a friend of the chief's.

Only one of Wehn's Chief Seattle fountains remains: this one, under the shadow of the totem pole in Pioneer Square. It is flanked by *Day/Night*, a 1991 artwork by Edgar Heap of Birds, which reads, in both English and Si'ahl's native Lushootseed, "Chief Seattle, now the streets are our home. Far away brothers and sisters we still remember you." The installation calls attention to the fact that Native Americans in King County are homeless at a rate three times that of the general population. Behind the statue across Yesler Way stands the Merchants Cafe, which opened in 1890. According to one of its current owners, it was known during the Klondike gold rush as the Sunday Bank, as miners who could not wait till Monday to do business at the banks or assay office could get cash on the spot for their gold. Reputedly the oldest restaurant in Seattle, the Merchants Cafe closed briefly in 2006 over a rent dispute, but has been operating without interruption ever since.

MADISON STREET

Streetcars are no longer tackling the grades of Madison Street

Left: Though this photograph is undated, the burned-out lot at the corner of Madison and Front streets attests to its having been taken after the 1889 fire. The presence of the Madison Street Cable Railway, heading up First Hill on its way to Madison Park on Lake Washington, further places it sometime after 1891. A car of the Front Street Cable Railway is visible at left. Running from King Street in Pioneer Square north to what is now Highland Drive on Queen Anne Hill, the line had the dubious distinction of being involved in Seattle's first public-transit death in 1889, when a car lost control descending Denny Hill and crashed a few blocks north of here. Prominent on the skyline are Providence Hospital (1882)—Seattle's first—at left, the public Central School (1889) at center, and the Rainier Hotel (1889) at right. The Queen City Bakery, in the foreground, echoes the nickname Seattle had carried since 1869.

Above: Nothing from the original shot remains in this present-day view up Madison Street from the corner of what is now First Avenue. The Rainier was demolished around 1910; the Central School was torn down in 1953, after being heavily damaged in the earthquake of 1949; and Providence Hospital relocated to what is now Cherry Hill in 1911. The brick building that once housed the Louvre restaurant was home to Warshal's Sporting Goods from 1936 to 2001, but was replaced in 2006 by Hotel 1000 and the Madison Tower condominiums. Across the street is the Henry M. Jackson Federal Building. The thirty-seven-story skyscraper was built in 1976 on the site of the 1891 Burke Building, and named for the U.S. senator on his death in 1983. Behind it are the Wells Fargo Center (1983), the Fourth and Madison Building (2002), and the Fifth and Madison condominium tower (2007).

FIRST METHODIST EPISCOPAL CHURCH / COLUMBIA CENTER

The Great Fire of 1889 managed to fall short of this Gothic Revival church; progress wasn't so accommodating

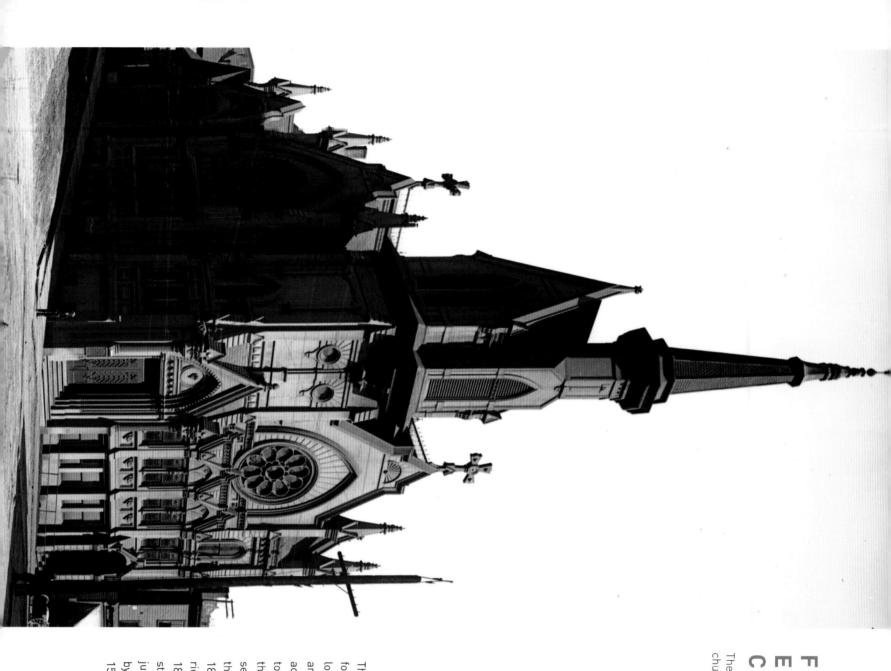

The First Methodist Episcopal Church, Seattle's first, was founded in 1853 by the Reverend David E. Blaine. It was first located in a white building at the southeast corner of Second and Columbia streets. At just over 860 square feet, it could accommodate a congregation of 150. Erected in 1855, it came to be called the "Little White Church"—the Methodist Protestant, Seattle's second house of worship. The church operated a school for the Chinese immigrants who began arriving in Seattle around 1860, and was threatened with arson during the anti-Chinese riots of 1886. Membership began to overtake capacity by the 1880s, and in 1887 construction began on this Gothic Revival structure at the southeast corner of Third and Marion streets, just north of the old site. Missing the Great Fire of June 1889 by mere blocks, the new church was dedicated on September 15 of that year.

With Seattle's rapid growth after the Klondike gold rush, the church needed larger quarters. In 1906 the old building was sold; in 1910 a new sanctuary, two blocks up the hill at the corner of Fifth Avenue and Marion Street, was dedicated. The congregation—now known as the First United Methodist Church of Seattle—would call that building home until 2007, when the church moved to Lower Queen Anne. This current view of the corner of Third and Marion shows the Columbia Center towering over the Central Building (1907), flanked on either side by the Seattle Municipal Tower (1990) and the Pacific Building (1970). Completed in 1985, the seventy-six-story Columbia Center is the tallest building in Seattle. At just over 932 feet tall, it is the twentieth-tallest in the United States. When it was built, it was the tallest building west of the Mississippi, and still ranks fourth. It is the second-tallest building on the West Coast, and has more stories than any skyscraper outside New York and Chicago.

KING STREET STATION

The station was modeled on Venice's Campanile di San Marco

Left: Seattle's first railroad was the Seattle and Walla Walla, started in 1874 in response to the Northern Pacific's having chosen Tacoma as its western terminus the year before. It only ever made it as far as Newcastle, a coal-mining town northeast of Renton. In 1880 Henry Villard of the Oregon Improvement Company bought the railroad and mines for $750,000, renaming the former the Columbia and Puget Sound Railroad (CPSRR). This photo, taken sometime between 1880 and 1882, shows the city's first true rail depot. It was built by the CPSRR in 1880 over what were then still the tidal flats of Elliott Bay at Piner's Point. This site was historically a winter camp of the local Duwamish tribe, and was marked as such on a map drawn by Lieutenant T. S. Phelps of the U.S. Navy during the 1856 Battle of Seattle.

Above: In 1881 Villard took over the Northern Pacific, and later connected Seattle to the transcontinental railroad. A local alliance between the Northern Pacific and the Great Northern Railway was discussed as early as 1893, but did not come to fruition until the end of the decade, when the two lines agreed to build a passenger station in Pioneer Square. King Street Station opened in May 1906, a year after the completion of a mile-long tunnel under downtown that helped alleviate traffic on Railroad Avenue. The building, with a clock tower inspired by Venice's Campanile di San Marco, was the tallest in Seattle until the 1914 completion of the Smith Tower. It was placed on the National Register of Historic Places in 1973. The city bought King Street Station from the BNSF Railway in 2008 for $10.

PORTAGE BAY

Golf has given way to university expansion on the shores of Portage Bay

This photo, taken around 1930 from the north slope of Capitol Hill, is centered on Portage Bay, named after the narrow isthmus between this arm of Lake Union and Union Bay. The Seattle Yacht Club is at center, just south and west of Montlake Park. Founded in 1892 in West Seattle, it moved to Portage Bay in 1920. On the far shore is the campus of the University of Washington, with the University Golf Course stretching from Fifteenth Avenue Northeast in the west to Husky Stadium in the east. Among the visible landmarks are Denny Hall (1895), the first building on this, the university's second campus; Suzzallo Library (1926); the Forestry Building, built for the 1909 Alaska-Yukon-Pacific Exposition but already condemned due to beetle damage; the smokestack of the university's power plant; and University Pavilion (1928). The Jensen Motor Boat Company sits at the foot of Fifteenth Avenue. In the distance are Ravenna Park, the Bryant neighborhood, and the Calvary Cemetery.

In 1933 the city condemned the land at bottom right—formerly a twenty-foot-deep peat bog, and then a dahlia farm—for the creation of Montlake Playfield. Thirty years later, a viaduct built as part of State Route 520 cut off the southern portion of Portage Bay. It is barely visible in this photograph, just below the Seattle Yacht Club, which was founded in 1892. The view north is dominated more than ever by the University of Washington, especially its South Campus. This is now home to the University of Washington Medical Center (1959) and Warren G. Magnuson Health Sciences Center (1947), as well as to the Department of Marine Sciences. The medical center houses the University of Washington School of Medicine. Perennially ranked number one in the nation for primary care and rural medicine, this research powerhouse is the only medical school serving five western states, and pioneered long-term kidney dialysis in the early 1960s.

FREMONT BRIDGE

Still in use as it approaches its centenary

In the late 1880s, the creek flowing from Lake Union to Salmon Bay was expanded into a small canal, and in 1892 a bridge was built to span it from Fremont to Queen Anne. The year before, the U.S. Army Corps of Engineers had begun to plan what would become the Lake Washington Ship Canal. As part of the construction that finally started twenty years later, the rickety bridge was demolished, with traffic diverted onto a pair of temporary structures for half a decade. The permanent bascule bridge that replaced them was the first of four the city built to span the Ship Canal, which was dedicated on July 4, 1917, the day this photo was taken. (The Fremont Bridge itself had opened a few weeks earlier, on June 15.) Here, the photographer is standing at its south end at the corner of Fourth Avenue North and Florentia Street.

Office parks rather than sawmills now flank the bridge's northern approach, replaced along with the southern one in 2007. It also now sports a two-tone coat of blue and orange, chosen as a compromise after a controversial vote during the 1985 Fremont Fair. Otherwise, the bridge looks much as it did on opening day. At only thirty feet above the Fremont Cut—at least twelve feet lower than the University Bridge—it is raised thirty-five times a day on average, making it one of the busiest drawbridges in the world. The Fremont Bridge ceased to be the main connection between Queen Anne and Fremont in 1932, when the high-level George Washington Memorial Bridge opened a few blocks to the east. Nevertheless, it carried 27,600 vehicles a day in 2008, with much of its northbound traffic destined for Ballard. The bridge became an official city landmark in 1981, and was added to the National Register of Historic Places in 1982.

LAKE UNION FROM CAPITOL HILL

Today boasting a community of houseboats almost 500 strong

Lake Union was named on July 4, 1854, when pioneer Thomas Mercer suggested it in anticipation of a canal connecting Hyas Chuck ("big water" in Chinook jargon) to Puget Sound via Tenas Chuck ("little water"). By the time this photo was taken in the 1920s from the west slope of Capitol Hill, that canal had been built, and Lake Union was bustling with marine activity. On the Eastlake shore are the Lake Union Dry Dock and Machine Works, at far left, and the cove, at far right, on which William Boeing built seaplanes in a hangar at the foot of Roanoke Street. The beginnings of a houseboat community can be seen extending south from Fairview Avenue. On the northern shore, the gasification plant of the Seattle Gas Light Company is just visible; to its west are the mills of Fremont and Ballard. Across the lake is Queen Anne Hill, the northeast slope of which has steep grades and is still largely wooded.

Lake Union is much less of a working lake than it once was, and is set to lose the Pacific Fleet of the National Oceanic and Atmospheric Administration in 2011, when it moves to Oregon. However, marine activity is still visible along its north shore, Lake Union Dry Dock is still in operation, and the houseboats now number just under 500. The gas plant closed in 1956 and is now a city park. The biggest change to the landscape is the George Washington Memorial Bridge. The first fixed span over the Lake Washington Ship Canal, it was built in 1932 as part of U.S. Route 99. The Aurora Bridge, as it is better known, is 2,945 feet long and 167 feet above the water, and was added to the National Register of Historic Places in 1982. Over 230 people have jumped from the bridge since 1932—according to some, it trails only San Francisco's Golden Gate Bridge in this regard. This led to the construction of a safety fence in 2010.

PROVIDENCE HOSPITAL / NAKAMURA COURTHOUSE

On the site of Seattle's first hospital now stands a federal courthouse

Left: This photo shows the Fifth Avenue side of Providence Hospital, which occupied the block bounded by Fifth and Sixth avenues and Madison and Spring streets. The hospital was founded by the Catholic Sisters of Charity of Providence, who had come to Seattle in 1877 to run the King County Poor Farm in Georgetown. Though intended for the indigent and located far away from the city center, it was the area's only healthcare facility, and was used by the rich and poor alike. Later that year, Mother Joseph moved the sisters into a house at the corner of Fifth and Madison. It quickly proved inadequate, and plans were drawn up—by Mother Joseph herself, with assistance from Donald McKay—for this building. Seattle's first purpose-built general hospital, it opened in 1882. The photo can have been taken no later than 1905, when construction of Seattle's Central Library began on the foreground lot.

Above: In 1907 the Providence Hospital School of Nursing opened here, but by 1911, Providence had outgrown Mother Joseph's building, and it moved to a new facility at the corner of Seventeenth Avenue and Jefferson Street. Providence merged with the Swedish Medical Center in 2000 and is now known as its Cherry Hill campus. In 1940 a federal courthouse was built on this lot. It served as the district courthouse until 2004, when a new one was built to the north. The Fifth and Madison courthouse, which was added to the National Register of Historic Places in 1980, was renovated from 2006 to 2009. It reopened as the William Kenzo Nakamura U.S. Courthouse, the local home of the Court of Appeals for the Ninth Circuit. Nakamura was a University of Washington student who was interned after Pearl Harbor. He subsequently joined the army and was killed in action in Italy while defending his platoon. His Distinguished Service Cross was upgraded to the Medal of Honor in 2000.

RAINIER BREWERY

Having survived Prohibition, the Rainier Brewery has now turned to coffee

Emil Sick may not have founded Rainier Beer or built its iconic Airport Way brewery, but his name will be forever linked with what many consider Seattle's quintessential beer. Rainier dates to 1883, when Andrew Hemrich and John Kopp built the Bay View Brewery next to a freshwater spring at the base of Beacon Hill. (The oft-mentioned 1878 date refers to an earlier brewery on the site.) In 1887 the building shown here was constructed at Ninth Avenue and Hanford Street. In 1893 Bay View merged with two other breweries and became the Seattle Brewing and Malting Company. That year, the Rainier brand was launched, and it soon became the largest brewery west of the Mississippi. When Washington went dry in 1916, Rainier moved its operations to California. After Prohibition was repealed in 1933, Emil Sick and his father took over Bay View. Two years later, he brought Rainier back to Seattle. By the time this photo was taken in 1939, the brewery was more successful than it had ever been.

Success continued apace at Rainier for decades. Meanwhile, Sick became president of the Seattle Historical Society and raised funds to build its Museum of History and Industry in 1952. He was also on the board of directors of the 1962 World's Fair. He passed away in 1964, and then in 1977 his heirs sold Rainier to a Wisconsin company. The brewery's fortunes began to turn in the 1980s, and by 1996 it was owned by Stroh. In 1999 Pabst bought the brand and closed the brewery, though the beer continues to be sold. Meanwhile, the iconic brewery itself—for decades topped by a red neon R— became the headquarters of Tully's Coffee, as well as home to artists' lofts and office and manufacturing space. The R was donated to the historical museum and replaced by a green T, but traffic reports still give conditions for Interstate 5 "at the brewery." The building's future is in some doubt due to contaminated paint applied in the 1960s, but its current owners are determined to preserve the landmark.

SEATTLE ART MUSEUM / SEATTLE ASIAN ART MUSEUM

The major attraction in Volunteer Park

Left: In 1876 the city paid J. M. Colman $2,000 for a forty-acre tract atop Capitol Hill. Eleven years later it became a park, first called Lake View, then simply City Park. In 1901 its name changed again, this time to Volunteer Park, after those who fought in the Spanish-American War. Two years later, the Olmsted brothers submitted a comprehensive plan for the city's parks and boulevards, including Volunteer Park; in this way, it gained formal gardens and a conservatory. In 1933 the park received its last major addition: the Seattle Art Museum (SAM). It was managed by the Art Institute of Seattle, whose predecessor organizations dated back to 1905. The building, designed by Carl F. Gould, founding head of the University of Washington School of Architecture, was donated to the city by the organization's president. The main shot, taken from the 1906 water tower, shows the museum and park in 1932, before the formal opening. The university campus is visible in the distance.

Above: The Art Moderne–style building, now an official city landmark, still stands in Volunteer Park, but no longer houses the museum's main collection. After eight years of planning, the SAM finally moved downtown in 1991, opening in a Robert Venturi–designed building at the corner of First Avenue and University Street. The Capitol Hill building was reopened as the Seattle Asian Art Museum in 1994, becoming the museum's second satellite site after the Modern Art Pavilion, which closed in 1987. The downtown museum expanded into the adjacent Russell Investments Center in 2007, and opened the Olympic Sculpture Park north of the central waterfront that same year. The SAM, which started with just under 2,000 objects, now has a collection of 23,000. The Asian Art Museum remains the main attraction in Volunteer Park, which during the summer is also a favorite spot for sunbathing, picnicking, and outdoor performances.

SAND POINT NAVAL AIR STATION / MAGNUSON PARK

Strategically important in World War II, the naval base declined after the Korean War

In 1918 Morgan Carkeek and his wife Emily donated twenty-three acres on Lake Washington's Pontiac Bay to the city for use as a children's park and campground. Around the same time, the military began eyeing the Sand Point peninsula as a possible airfield. King County began developing the adjacent tracts, and the first flight took place in 1921. In 1922 the navy began its own construction. Sand Point made world history in 1924 when it served as the start and finish of the first aerial circumnavigation of the world. Two years later, the installation, along with Carkeek Park and most of the rest of the peninsula, was transferred without charge to the U.S. Navy, and the Sand Point Naval Air Station was established. A new Carkeek Park was established on Puget Sound, and the campground was moved to O. O. Denny Park near Kirkland. Shown here in June 1939 is one of the Aircraft Scouting Force's flying boats, thirty of which arrived at Sand Point that year.

Sand Point grew considerably during World War II. After the war, its strength was reduced from 8,000 to 3,000 personnel. In 1950 it was scheduled for closure. The Korean War put these plans on hold, but when it ended in 1953, Sand Point became part of the Naval Reserve, and operated at less than 3 percent of its World War II strength. Air operations ended permanently in 1970 and the navy gave up nearly three quarters of the property, keeping the rest as a support station. The city acquired two thirds of the surplus, with the National Oceanic and Atmospheric Administration (NOAA) receiving the remainder. In 1975 the former airfield became Sand Point Park, and in 1977 it was renamed after U.S. senator Warren G. Magnuson. The base was completely closed in 1991, and the city expanded Magnuson Park's boundaries to include the support buildings. The hangars are now divided between the NOAA and the park. Some remain vacant, while others play host to sporting events and book sales.

FORT LAWTON / DISCOVERY PARK

The U.S. Army offered it to the city for a dollar, but was turned down

Left: The Puget Sound Naval Shipyard was established in Bremerton in 1891 and required coastal artillery for its defense. Seven years later, the citizens of Seattle donated just over 700 acres of the Magnolia peninsula to the War Department for this purpose. Fort Lawton, named for a general killed in the Spanish-American War, was activated on February 9, 1900. Never the major installation it was envisioned to be, the fort welcomed the U.S. Army Corps of Engineers in the 1920s, and in 1938 it was offered to the city as surplus for the price of $1. Unwilling to take on the tract's maintenance, the city turned down the offer. With the declaration of war three years later, Fort Lawton became a prisoner-of-war camp and part of the Seattle Port of Embarkation. The inset is of German prisoners of war being paraded past the post theater toward the end of World War II; the main shot shows one of the Nike missiles that were installed at Fort Lawton in the 1950s.

Above: In the 1960s, Fort Lawton was again declared surplus, then briefly proposed as the location of an antiballistic missile base. After this proposal was withdrawn in 1968, the city set about reacquiring the land. The city took title to over half the property in 1972, with parts reserved for a Native American cultural center and a wastewater treatment plant. It was dedicated as Discovery Park the next year. This name honored Captain George Vancouver's ship, the HMS *Discovery*, which explored the area in 1792. More of the fort was surplused over the years; the park—Seattle's largest—eventually grew to 534 acres. The army has retained a portion for its cemetery and some reserve operations. Some of the old buildings, seen here, have been preserved as part of the Fort Lawton Historic District; otherwise, the grounds have largely reverted to their native state, and are a popular hiking destination.

UNOCAL SITE / OLYMPIC SCULPTURE PARK

A former industrial site has been transformed into a cultural landmark

Though not often mentioned in the same breath as Teapot Dome, Oil City, or Spindletop, Seattle and western Washington have a long history with the petroleum industry. Drilling began in the area in the early 1880s; most wells came up dry. Yet due to its status as an up-and-coming port, large quantities of oil, gas, and diesel nevertheless made their way through Seattle. One candidate for the world's first gas station was established here in 1907. Operated by Standard Oil of California, it was located at Holgate Street and Whatcom Avenue in the Industrial District south of downtown. Around that time, Union Oil of California purchased land at the northern end of the central waterfront, on either side of Elliott Avenue between Broad and Bay streets. There, next to the tracks of the Great Northern Railway, it built a distribution center and tank farm. It is seen here in early 1941.

After a fiery accident on the Alaskan Way Viaduct involving a Unocal tanker truck, most operations at the facility ceased in 1975. Unocal closed its offices in 1986 and began demolition soon after. For the next twenty-one years, the property stood vacant and was an eyesore in marked contrast to the neighboring Myrtle Edwards Park, the tourist-oriented central waterfront, and the Seattle Center. In 1996 discussions began regarding the creation of a new outdoor sculpture park for the city. Three years later, a proposal was submitted to build it on the Unocal site. The Olympic Sculpture Park finally opened in 2007 as part of the Seattle Art Museum.

UNIVERSITY DISTRICT

This fourteen-story Art Deco hotel was sponsored by a neighborhood committee

Left: This undated photo was taken from Brooklyn Avenue Northeast just south of Forty-fifth Street in the University District. Based on the presence of the streetcar and the vintage of the cars, it was likely taken in the early 1930s, not too long after the Edmond Meany Hotel (1931) and Brooklyn Building (1929) were constructed. The Art Deco/Modernist hotel was sponsored by a neighborhood committee, which raised nearly a million dollars for site acquisition and construction. Robert Reamer, its architect, also designed Seattle's Olympic Hotel, Skinner Building, Fifth Avenue Theater, and the 1411 Fourth Avenue building, all downtown. The Meany was named in a community contest. Its honoree, Edmond S. Meany, was born in 1862 and died in 1935. He was a University of Washington professor, state legislator, and founder of the *Washington Historical Quarterly*. At fourteen floors, the Meany was for years the tallest building in the area.

Above: In the 1990s, its name was changed to the Meany Tower Hotel, and then the University Tower Hotel. It is now known as the Hotel Deca, and remains the most prominent lodging establishment north of the Ship Canal. Across Forty-fifth Avenue now stands the twenty-two-story University of Washington Plaza, also known as the UW Tower. The General Insurance Company of America, which had moved into the Brooklyn Building in 1936, became Safeco Corporation in 1968. Five years later it built what was then known as Safeco Plaza on the site. The skyscraper, designed by the local firm NBBJ, was and is the tallest building outside of downtown. In 2006 Safeco sold its headquarters to the University of Washington for $130 million. The tower complex now houses more than twenty university departments.

PACIFIC MEDICAL CENTER

The onetime home of Seattle success story Amazon.com

Left: This photo shows the Marine Hospital on Beacon Hill nearing completion in 1932. The sixteen-story Art Deco edifice occupies twelve acres at the northern end of the hill, donated to the U.S. Public Health Service by the city in 1928. The house of M. Harwood Young, who named Beacon Hill after the hill in his hometown of Boston, once stood in the area. The design is credited to John Graham Sr. and the firm of Carl F. Gould and Charles H. Bebb, thus bringing together three titans of Seattle architecture. Graham designed the 1913 Ford plant on Lake Union, the 1919 Frederick and Nelson Building, the 1921 Seattle Yacht Club, the 1924 Dexter Horton Building, the 1930 Exchange Building, and many others. In addition to the campus of the University of Washington, Bebb and Gould designed the 1924 Seattle Times Building and the 1916 administration building at the Ship Canal Locks in Ballard. Gould founded the University of Washington's Department of Architecture in 1914 and served as its head until 1926.

Above: In 1951 the Marine Hospital became the Public Health Service Hospital, and in 1979 it was placed on the National Register of Historic Places. Two years later, the federal government shut down the hospital system. The city then chartered the Pacific Hospital Preservation and Development Authority (PHPDA), which ran the hospital until 1987. The bulk of the building stood vacant for the next eleven years. During that time, it underwent renovation and seismic stabilization, including the additions seen here. In 1998 the federal government, which still owned the building now known as the Pacific Medical Center, allowed the PHPDA to lease it to a developer, using the proceeds to fund uncompensated health care. That developer sublet the tower to Amazon.com, which made the top fourteen floors its headquarters for the next decade. The Pacific Medical Center's flagship clinic still occupies the ground floor, while Amazon has moved its headquarters to South Lake Union.

INTERSTATE 5

Not every building could get out of the way of Interstate 5

When the George Washington Memorial Bridge opened in 1932, the route of the Pacific Highway—U.S. Highway 99—through Seattle was complete. Yet by 1951 there were already calls for a supplemental expressway to the east. The Seattle Freeway was approved in 1955 and became part of the Interstate Highway System on its creation in 1956. North of Capitol Hill, its route would "traverse residential areas entirely." Seen here is one of those residential areas in 1958. This is the corner of East Fiftieth Street and Seventh Avenue Northeast in the University District, just blocks north of the first section of the freeway to be built—the Ship Canal Bridge. Some buildings, like this one, were moved. But most of the 4,500 condemned parcels fell to the wrecking ball, forever changing neighborhoods and separating downtown from First Hill and Capitol Hill, the University District from Wallingford, and Roosevelt from Green Lake.

The 4,429-foot-long Ship Canal Bridge, seen here in the distance beyond Northeast Forty-fifth Street, opened in 1962. Interstate 5 was completed through Seattle by 1967. It is used by all sorts of traffic, and even with reversible express lanes is the site of mile-long backups. According to the Washington State Department of Transportation, average daily traffic on the interstate is 280,000 vehicles—including 50,000 buses and 12,000 trucks—and the freeway has been used by over three billion vehicles since its completion. Its design capacity was long ago surpassed, but there is little room for growth, as construction through residential neighborhoods is no longer politically acceptable, and expansion in the commercial core is as good as physically impossible. This, along with overcrowding on Interstates 405 and 90 and State Route 520, has earned Seattle a permanent place on the annual lists of most-congested metro areas.

SEARS / STARBUCKS CENTER

From an iconic retailer of the twentieth century to a star brand of the twenty-first

Sears, Roebuck and Company was synonymous with American retail for nearly 100 years after its founding in Minneapolis in 1886 as the R. W. Sears Watch Company. In 1912 the Chicago, Milwaukee, St. Paul and Pacific Railroad—which, along with the Union Pacific, had just erected Union Station south of Pioneer Square—hoped to increase its traffic, and built the country's premier mail-order general merchandiser a new facility at the corner of Utah Avenue and Lander Street. This land had previously been part of the Elliott Bay tidal flats, but was filled in as far east as Beacon Hill with the spoils of Seattle's many regrades, and now stood as a large industrial district. Sears, which greatly expanded the building in 1915, used it for its first distribution center outside of Chicago as well as its regional headquarters. It is seen here in 1918.

Sears began opening retail stores in 1925, and one soon appeared in this building. Other area stores were established in Roosevelt and Ballard. Sears enjoyed continued success until the 1980s, but as catalog sales began to drop off, the large distribution center became a liability. It finally closed in 1987, though Sears maintains a retail store in part of the building. Three years later, developers Nitze-Stagen, who had also purchased and renovated Union Station, acquired the tower, which stood as the second-largest building by square feet in the Pacific Northwest. They renamed it the Sodo Center for its location south of the Kingdome stadium. In 1997 the Sodo Center became the Starbucks Center when the coffee chain, founded in 1971 at Pike Place Market, made the building its headquarters and topped it with its iconic mermaid. The Sears store, at eighty-five years old, is said to be the longest-operating in the country.

GREEN LAKE AQUA THEATER

Led Zeppelin has played here, but the stage hasn't remained the same

Left: Though many think Green Lake is man-made, it was actually carved out by the same Vashon Glacier responsible for Lakes Washington and Union. Named in 1855 for its algal bloom, the lake saw its first white settler in 1869. In 1891 the Fremont streetcar reached Green Lake's shores, and the same year the surrounding neighborhood was annexed to Seattle. Green Lake was a part of the parks and boulevards plan the Olmsted brothers prepared for the city in 1903. As such, in 1911 it was lowered seven feet to create extra parkland, and ringed with a boulevard. (This had the side effect of drying up the western half of Ravenna Creek, which formerly drained Green Lake into Lake Washington.) The lake and park became a recreational magnet, and the neighborhood flourished. In 1950 an outdoor theater was built on the lake's south shore. Featuring a floating stage, the Aqua Theater played host to water follies, plays, musicals, concerts, and comedians. It is shown here during a performance in the summer of 1961.

Above: The Aqua Theater began a slow decline thereafter, losing the follies in 1964. Though Three Dog Night, Led Zeppelin, and the Grateful Dead would play there in 1969, the latter's show proved to be the last one in the facility. Over the next decade, the stage and most of the grandstand were demolished and replaced by a small craft center now home to Green Lake Crew, one of the parks department's rowing programs. The remaining stands are now used for stair-running, and also provide an excellent view of the north shore, which can be reached by a 2.8-mile circular path. The park now includes two bathing beaches, an island wildlife refuge, the Seattle Public Theater at the Bathhouse, a community center, a swimming pool, a wading pool, and sports fields. Racing shells, rented paddle boats, canoes, and kayaks ply the water, while motorized vehicles are forbidden. Fishing for trout and carp off the lake's many docks is another popular pastime.

BALLARD LOCKS

Providing a buffer zone between freshwater and salt water

Pioneer Thomas Mercer named Lake Union in 1854, anticipating it would one day connect Lake Washington in the east to Puget Sound in the west. The U.S. Navy, which was considering a freshwater shipyard on Lake Washington, gave its blessing to such a plan in 1867, but when the yard was finally built in 1891, it was in Bremerton. That same year, however, planning for the canal began under the aegis of the U.S. Army Corps of Engineers. A route via Union Bay, Portage Bay, Lake Union, Salmon Bay, and Shilshole Bay was approved in 1900, and work on the canal started in 1911. A set of locks was built in the middle of Salmon Bay to prevent salt water from infiltrating the lakes and to maintain their water level. The Lake Washington Ship Canal and the Ballard Locks opened on July 4, 1917. This photo from October 1939 shows a pontoon for the Lake Washington Floating Bridge on its way to being installed. The Great Northern Railway's Salmon Bay Bridge, built in 1914, is in the background.

The locks were named after district engineer Hiram M. Chittenden in 1956, and the plantings behind the administration building were named the Carl S. English Jr. Botanical Gardens in 1968. Along with the rest of the canal, the locks were added to the National Register of Historic Places in 1978. They see more than two million tons of cargo a year, though the majority of the 60,000 vessels making the passage are pleasure craft, kayaks, and the like. The locks can raise or lower a vessel as much as twenty-six feet in fifteen minutes. The Fishermen's Terminal, home to the North Pacific fishing fleet, is just east of the locks, as is the Ballard-Interbay industrial district. The old fish ladder was rebuilt in 1976, and its underwater viewing windows, along with the locks and gardens themselves, are a major tourist attraction. The 1916 administration building (right) was designed by Carl F. Gould, most notable for his plan of the University of Washington campus.

VIEW FROM BEACON HILL

Showing the early settlement before the 1889 fire

Above: This photograph, taken in 1883 or 1884 from the north end of Beacon Hill, shows a young Seattle—the first white settlers had arrived just over thirty years previously, and the city itself was not yet twenty—still conforming largely to its original topography. At center left is Pioneer Square, the original city center, abutting onto open water at its southern end. The forested Magnolia peninsula is in the distance, and in front of it is Denny Hill, which rises as high as 240 feet. There is as yet little development east of Sixth Street, though here the forest has long since been logged. At upper right is the Territorial University of Washington, founded in 1861 on Denny's Knoll. At center right is what appears to be, under construction, the second building of Holy Names Academy. The Catholic girls' school was founded in 1880 at Second and Seneca streets, and moved to Seventh and Jackson in 1884.

Right: This modern view, taken from José Rizal Park at the north end of the East Duwamish Greenbelt, is one of the canonical images of the city, appearing in everything from postcards and guidebooks to Web sites and news backdrops. Pioneer Square is largely obscured by the Chinatown/International District, which became a federal historic district in 1987. Unlike many other such neighborhoods, Chinatown is still mostly Asian. It has a solid Filipino and Vietnamese population in addition to the Chinese, whose presence in Seattle dates to the early 1860s. In the foreground, Interstate 5 and its interchange with Interstate 90 cut a wide swath through downtown, furthering the topographic changes that came with the regrading of Jackson and Dearborn streets in the early 1900s. Notable structures on the skyline, from west to east, are the Smith Tower (1914), the 1201 Third Avenue Tower (1988), the Columbia Center (1985), the Seattle Municipal Tower (1990), Two Union Square (1989), and, across the freeway, the Harborview Medical Center (1931).

JAPANTOWN AND YESLER TERRACE

Seattle's Japanese neighborhood was displaced by public housing

Left: The Chinese were the first Asians to move to Seattle in appreciable numbers, beginning in the 1860s. In fact, they were the first immigrants of any nationality after the white pioneers. They were soon followed by Japanese and Filipinos, many coming via Hawaii. Nihonmachi, or Japantown, soon sprang up north of Chinatown along Yesler Way and Main and Washington streets, and by 1901 there was a large enough community to form the Seattle Buddhist Church, which began that year in a rented house at Sixth Avenue and Main Street. According to temple archives, the November 15 opening was the first Jodo Shinshu Buddhist service in the entire Pacific Northwest. Seven years later, the temple moved to its own building at Tenth Avenue and Main Street. It is shown here in 1914.

Above: In 1939 the Seattle Housing Authority was established as part of the New Deal. That December, it received $3 million to build a 700-unit, forty-three-acre public housing project atop First Hill. Yesler Terrace, as it was named, was to be the first racially integrated public housing project in the country. However, it was planned for the area around the intersection of Yesler Way and Broadway. The eastern half of Japantown therefore had to be condemned. The church moved a few blocks east on Main, to Fourteenth Avenue, and opened its new building in October 1941. But after Pearl Harbor, Seattle's largest minority community was sent to internment camps. The building was used by the government until 1946. Designated a city landmark thirty years later, it still houses what is now the Seattle Buddhist Temple. There are still many Japanese in Seattle, though no longer concentrated in Japantown, which was further encroached upon by the construction of Interstate 5 in the 1960s.

UNIVERSITY OF WASHINGTON METROPOLITAN TRACT

The old building is long gone, but the Ionic columns were salvaged

Left: The Territorial University of Washington opened on November 4, 1861, on a ten-acre tract overlooking downtown Seattle known as Denny's Knoll. Donated to the state by pioneers Arthur Denny, Edward Lander, and Charles Terry, it was bounded by what were to be Union, Seneca, Fourth, and Sixth streets. The university, which then also taught grade and secondary school, had an inaugural class of thirty. Its president and sole faculty member was twenty-two-year-old Asa Shinn Mercer, soon to become famous for recruiting single women from the East Coast to rectify Seattle's frustrating gender disparity. In 1874 the university enrolled its first black student. Two years later, it awarded its first bachelor's degree to Clara Antoinette McCarty, in science. This photograph shows the building sometime in the mid-1880s. The school became the University of Washington when the territory became a state in 1889.

Above: In 1894 construction began on a new campus north of Portage Bay; the first two buildings opened in 1895 and 1902. The university now has more than 500 buildings serving nearly 50,000 students, and enjoys a high national and worldwide ranking. The downtown building was used for various purposes until 1908, when it was demolished. Its columns were salvaged and now stand in the Sylvan Grove Theater on the main campus. Meanwhile, the regents decided to lease the old grounds for development. In 1907 this lease came into the hands of the Metropolitan Improvement Company, and the blocks became known as the Metropolitan Tract. In 2008 state revenue from the tract stood at $8 million. This present-day view looks up University Street from Fifth Avenue. At right is the 1924 Fairmont Olympic Hotel, designed by Bebb and Gould, who also planned the university campus. Across the street stands the Rainier Tower. Built in 1977, it was designed by Minoru Yamasaki of World Trade Center fame. The tapering base stands eleven full stories.

SEATTLE CENTRAL LIBRARY

Starting a tradition of grand library buildings serving Seattle

Above: The Seattle Public Library can date its founding to 1868 and the creation of the Seattle Library Foundation. Its first lending library opened in 1869, but it wasn't until 1890 that the library became a city department. From 1891 to 1899 it operated out of Pioneer Square's Occidental Building. That year it moved into a mansion built by pioneer Henry Yesler, who had died in 1892. This building burned in 1901, and the library was forced to find a new home. Soon thereafter, philanthropist Andrew Carnegie pledged $200,000 for a grand Central Library. The block bounded by Madison and Spring streets and Fourth and Fifth avenues was cleared, and construction began in 1905. The Beaux Arts sandstone building designed by Peter J. Weber opened in December 1906, and is seen here in 1914 from the corner of Fourth and Madison.

Right: Over the subsequent years, the Seattle Public Library system grew. With Carnegie's help, new branches were added in West Seattle, Green Lake, the University District, Queen Anne, Columbia City, and Fremont. In the 1950s, the Central Library was deemed in need of replacement, and was demolished in 1957. Its replacement was an International Style structure that was considered the height of modernity, complete with a drive-through window and what is said to have been the country's first escalator in a library. At quadruple its predecessor's size, it served the city's needs from 1960 to 2004, when it too was replaced. The new building, seen here from the same corner, cost $155.5 million and was funded by the 1998 Libraries for All bond measure, at the time the nation's largest. Designed by famed Dutch architect Rem Koolhaas, it is more than half as large again as the 1960 structure.

SEATTLE POST-INTELLIGENCER BUILDING

A casualty of media fragmentation continues online

On December 10, 1863, J. R. Watson published the first issue of the Seattle Gazette, the young town's first newspaper. It folded in 1867 and was resurrected as the Weekly Intelligencer in August of that year. In June 1876, it became the Daily Intelligencer. In October 1878, future mayor John Leary founded the Post, which merged with the earlier paper on October 1, 1881, creating the Seattle Post-Intelligencer. Ten years later, the Seattle Press-Times, later called the Seattle Daily Times and then simply the Seattle Times, was founded. William Randolph Hearst bought the Post-Intelligencer in 1921, adding the morning paper to his growing empire. In 1936 Franklin D. Roosevelt's son-in-law John Boettiger became publisher; FDR's daughter Anna became assistant editor. They departed in 1943. In 1948 the Post-Intelligencer moved into a new building at the corner of Sixth Avenue and Wall Street. On its roof was placed a globe, thirty feet in diameter and over eighteen tons in weight. Topped by an eagle, it proclaimed "It's in the P-I" in large red neon letters.

The *Post-Intelligencer* and *Times* settled into a duopoly for the next sixty-one years. This arrangement was formalized in 1983 with the establishment of a joint operating agreement. The *Post-Intelligencer* would maintain a newsroom and editorial board, but all other aspects of newspaper production would thereafter be handled by the *Times*. No longer in need of large facilities, the *Post-Intelligencer* moved, along with its globe, to an office building on Elliott Avenue West. The agreement lasted without incident until 2000, when the *Times* switched from afternoons to mornings, directly competing with the *Post-Intelligencer*. That same year, the Pacific Northwest Newspaper Guild went on a nearly two-month strike. This, combined with the ascendancy of Internet media, caused the Hearst Corporation to begin suffering annual losses; on March 17, 2009, the paper printed its last edition, after Hearst was unable to find a buyer. Its Web site has continued to operate since then, with a greatly reduced staff. Initial traffic, even without a companion print edition, has been encouraging. This view looks southwest at the *Post-Intelligencer* offices from the vicinity of the Seattle Center. Beyond, one of Washington State Ferries' vessels can be seen heading for Colman Dock; in the background are Harbor Island and the West Seattle Bridge.

EAGLES AUDITORIUM

The fraternal organization for men in arts and entertainment started in Seattle

Left: On February 6, 1898, six Seattle theater owners—among them national impresarios John Cort and John Considine—founded the Order of Good Things, a fraternal organization for men in arts and entertainment. The group's name was soon changed to the Fraternal Order of Eagles. Its growth, attributable to touring performers, was rapid, reaching 350,000 members by 1908, with 1,800 aeries (lodges) across North America. A past president of the organization is credited with first proposing Mother's Day in 1904, and Theodore Roosevelt and Warren G. Harding were among the first U.S. presidents to be members. In 1924 the Eagles built a grand "Mother Aerie" at the corner of Seventh Avenue and Union Street in downtown Seattle. Pictured here in 1926, it was designed by Henry Bittman, whose firm was also responsible for the Decatur Building (1921) and Terminal Sales Building (1923).

Above: The Eagles' success continued for many years, counting FDR and Presidents Truman, Kennedy, Carter, and Reagan among its subsequent members. However, the general decline in membership among fraternal organizations took its toll. By the 1970s, the Eagles had left their grand building for smaller quarters, first in Georgetown, then in Maple Leaf, where the current Mother Aerie stands on Lake City Way Northeast. The building stood vacant for many years, landing on the National Register of Historic Places in 1983 and becoming a city landmark in 1985. In 1994 ACT—founded in 1965 as A Contemporary Theatre and now one of Seattle's leading houses—took possession, along with the nonprofit Housing Resource Group. After much renovation, the building reopened in 1996. In addition to four theaters and support services, Kreielsheimer Place—named for local arts patron Leo Kreielsheimer—also contains forty-four units of low-income housing.

LAKE UNION STEAM PLANT

From generating steam to becoming a powerhouse of biotech innovation

Left: This photo was taken in the summer of 1937 and shows Seattle City Light and Power's Plant No. 3, built twenty-three years earlier. The coal-fired steam plant was designed by city architect Daniel Huntington, who, in addition to ten fire stations and the Fremont Branch Library, also designed the Delamar Apartments and Rainier Chapter House of the Daughters of the American Revolution. The Lake Union Steam Plant, as it was known, was built on the southeastern shore of Lake Union just west of Eastlake Avenue; this portion of Fairview Avenue, seen here looking south, is actually a low bridge. City Light, founded in 1890 as the Department of Lighting and Water Works, had been operating hydroelectric projects on area rivers since 1905, but Seattle still relied on fossil fuels for much of its generative capacity, both here and at the privately owned steam plant in Georgetown.

Above: In 1951 City Light bought out all private operators within the city limits. Though its reliance on hydroelectric power grew—today nearly 90 percent of Seattle's electricity comes from that source—the steam plant on Lake Union remained in operation for thirty-three more years. After pollution concerns forced its closure in 1984, it stood vacant for the better part of a decade while redevelopment and remediation were worked through. Finally, in 1993, the local biotechnology firm ZymoGenetics acquired the property for its new headquarters. The unstable smokestacks were replaced by replicas and moved to the Eastlake Avenue side, and the plant became a city landmark the next year. The Lake Union Steam Plant stands today as one of the city's most notable examples of adaptive reuse. It was a harbinger of changes to the South Lake Union neighborhood, which has been transformed from a low-rise industrial neighborhood to a world center of biomedical sciences.

EVERGREEN POINT FLOATING BRIDGE

The longest floating bridge in the world

Left: With the opening of the Lake Washington Floating Bridge from Seattle to Mercer Island in 1940, the Madison Park–Kirkland ferry's days were numbered. Yet once the ferry *Leschi* made its last run in August 1950, there was no longer a direct link from Seattle to the northern Eastside. A 1956 plan called for the construction of a second bridge from the Sand Point Naval Air Station to Juanita, northwest of Kirkland. However, the alignment ultimately chosen was from Montlake to Medina, as part of State Route 520. The highway would run through a residential neighborhood and sensitive wetlands in Portage and Union bays, as well as cross Marsh and Foster islands. These were part of the Washington Park Arboretum; Foster Island had once been a Native American burial ground. Despite all this, construction began in 1960. Shown here is the west end of the bridge in 1962, the year before it opened.

Above: The Evergreen Point Floating Bridge, which opened in 1963, was later officially named for Governor Albert D. Rosellini. At 7,578 feet, it is the longest of its kind in the world, having surpassed the bridge to Mercer Island. Ramps were built to a proposed north-south freeway that would have taken out even more of the Arboretum, but the R. H. Thomson Expressway, named for the early twentieth-century city engineer, faced stiff public opposition. It and other such projects, including a resurrection of the northern bridge proposal, were all canceled by 1977. Today, the four-lane bridge is in dire need of replacement. Operating at nearly double its capacity, it has no room for mass transit, and is at risk during heavy storms and earthquakes. The Department of Transportation has given it until 2017; meanwhile, the long process continues of deciding on a replacement design acceptable to all parties.

MOUNT BAKER TUNNELS

Portals of the North Pacific

Left: Lake Washington, around twenty miles from the Sammamish River in the north to the Cedar River in the south, was a barrier to Seattle's eastward expansion. The Sunset Highway, the state's main east–west route, was forced to detour around the south end via Renton. Direct access to the Eastside was provided by ferries, which sailed from the docks at Madison and Leschi parks. In 1921 engineer Homer M. Hadley proposed a floating bridge for the glacial lake, which had a muddy bottom and was as deep as 214 feet, making it unsuitable for conventional construction. In 1937 this plan was approved, and the Lake Washington Floating Bridge opened on July 2, 1940. Then the world's longest such bridge at 6,620 feet, it ran from Seattle's Mount Baker neighborhood to Mercer Island. To bring U.S. Highway 10 into downtown, twin tunnels were built under Mount Baker. Their eastern entrance is shown here in 1945, proclaiming the city of Seattle the "Portal of the North Pacific."

Above: After the Interstate Highway System was established in 1956, Interstate 90 replaced U.S. 10. As the Eastside suburbs grew, traffic began to worsen on the bridge, which was renamed in 1967 after Lacey V. Murrow, who was director of highways when it was built. A parallel bridge, this one named for Hadley, opened in 1989, and the 1940 bridge was converted to carry eastbound traffic only. During renovation in 1990, it sank spectacularly after a Thanksgiving weekend storm. A replacement bridge, in the same alignment, opened in 1993. A pedestrian and bicycle trail now parallels the freeway. Part of the Mountains to Sound Greenway, which stretches from Seattle to the Cascade Range, it runs over the bridge from Beacon Hill in Seattle to Eastgate in Bellevue. Extensions west to Elliott Bay and east to Lake Sammamish remain unfunded.

MONTLAKE CUT

College crews race up the Montlake Cut on opening day

Left: Portage Bay, the eastern arm of Lake Union, was named after the portage that was required to bring goods over the isthmus that separated it from Union Bay. It was a natural location for a cut, which was discussed as early as 1854. Harvey Pike, who had planned Union City just to the south, made abortive attempts at a canal in the early 1860s, but even after expansion in the 1880s, it was only ever wide enough to transport logs. The U.S. Army Corps of Engineers began planning for a proper canal in 1891. Twenty years later, the digging began. The Montlake Cut, named for the neighborhood that grew up on the Union City plat, is shown here under construction around 1914. The photographer is standing on the northern bank looking southwest; Portage Bay is just visible at far right. Adelphia Hall, built in 1905 as the first building of Seattle College High School on its new campus, can be seen atop Capitol Hill at left.

Above: The Montlake Cut, along with the rest of the Lake Washington Ship Canal, officially opened on July 4, 1917, though shipping traffic began to come through the year before. Planning for a bridge had begun in 1914, but a permanent crossing would not open until 1925. This view is from that bridge, which carries Montlake Boulevard forty-eight feet above the water to the campus of the University of Washington. It was taken on opening day—the beginning of the local boating season, which is always the first Saturday in May. A Seattle tradition since 1920, it features a parade of boats sponsored by the Seattle Yacht Club, located a few blocks to the south. Opening day is capped off by a collegiate crew race known since 1987 as the Windermere Cup. It has historically been dominated by the University of Washington, whose shell house is on the northern bank.

WORLD'S FAIR / SEATTLE CENTER

Still a center for education and leisure, fifty years on

Left: Seattle's second world's fair took place from April 21 to October 21, 1962, on land that had once been considered for a civic center. Ten million people came to the space-age Century 21 Exposition, which was originally planned for 1959, the fiftieth anniversary of the Alaska-Yukon-Pacific Exposition on the University of Washington campus. Modernist architect Paul Thiry designed the grounds. Shown here is a leg of its landmark tower, the futuristic, 605-foot-tall Space Needle, which itself drew over two million visitors. To its south are various pavilions, including those of General Electric, electric utilities, the new state of Alaska, the gas industry, and the Ford Motor Company. On the other side of the Needle are exhibits on commerce, fashion, and interiors. The corner of the Bell System's building is at far right.

Above: The fairgrounds are now known as the Seattle Center. In addition to the Space Needle, the Pacific Science Center, Experience Music Project, Science Fiction Museum and Hall of Fame, Seattle Repertory Theatre, Intiman Theatre, Seattle Opera, Seattle Children's Theatre, KeyArena, and Memorial Stadium are counted among its attractions. It has also hosted the Bite of Seattle food festival since 1986 and the Bumbershoot and Northwest Folklife cultural festivals since 1971 and 1972, respectively. In the 1980s, Disney submitted a redevelopment plan for the campus that would have demolished numerous landmarks and commercialized the grounds, but public opposition was vehement. There has, however, been talk of demolishing the stadium and converting the Fun Forest amusement park into a privately run glass museum. The privately owned Space Needle, which became an official city landmark in 1999, got a new ground-level pavilion in 2000, and remains Seattle's most recognizable structure.

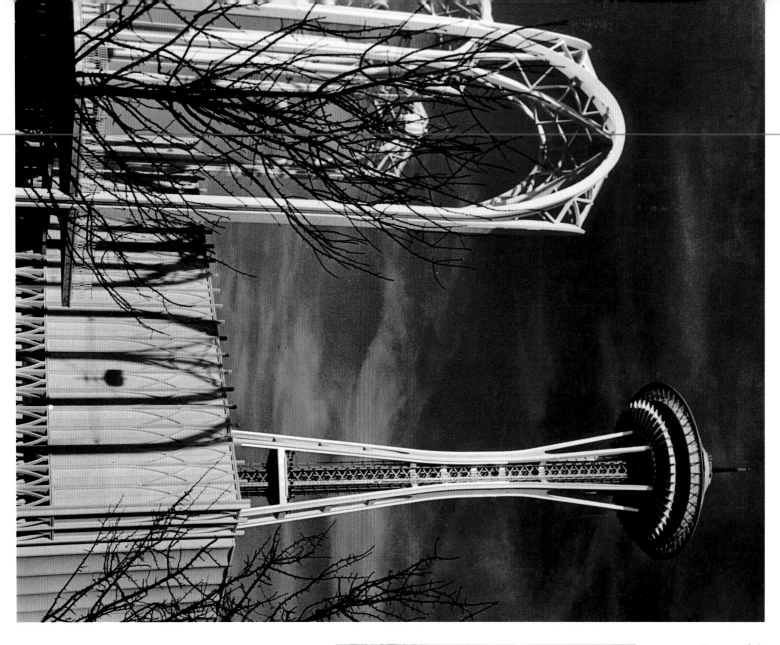

SPACE NEEDLE / PACIFIC SCIENCE CENTER

Modernist legacies of the Century 21 Exposition

Two of Seattle's most iconic landmarks are captured in this shot, taken sometime during the 1962 Century 21 Exposition. At right is the 605-foot-tall Space Needle, which became the tallest structure west of the Mississippi upon its completion. Privately owned, the futuristic tower cost $4.5 million to build, and features an observation deck at 520 feet, with a revolving restaurant twenty feet below. The Space Needle alone drew over two million fair visitors out of ten million total. Its primary architect, John Graham, was one of the five developers who formed the Pentagram Corporation after government funding fell through. The inset shows the top of the tower with its original Galaxy Gold paint job. In the foreground of the main image is the United States Science Pavilion, with its "space gothic" arches. A cornerstone of the exposition, whose focus was on science and technology, the six-building complex was designed by Minoru Yamasaki. A Seattle native and University of Washington graduate, Yamasaki practiced in New York and Detroit from the 1930s to the 1950s. Before the Science Pavilion, his best-known work was the 1955 Pruitt-Igoe public-housing project in St. Louis.

The Space Needle remained the tallest structure in town until 1969, when it was surpassed by the 1001 Fourth Avenue Plaza. It is still the sixth-tallest in the city, and the third-tallest observation tower in the United States. The 100-foot SkyLine level was built in 1982, and renovations and additional construction took place during 1999 and 2000. Still privately owned, it became an official city landmark in 1999. The day after the Century 21 Exposition closed, the United States Science Pavilion reopened as the Pacific Science Center, a nonprofit science museum. Most of the original exhibits have been replaced, though a few remain. In addition to its two IMAX theaters and attractions such as the Tropical Butterfly House, Science Playground, and a colony of naked mole rats, the Science Center has played host to major traveling exhibitions, beginning with 1984's China: 7,000 Years of Discovery, as well as its own Discovering the Dead Sea Scrolls in 2006. Yamasaki, who went on to design two other buildings in Seattle, is best known today for designing the twin towers of the World Trade Center.

RAINIER VALLEY RAIL

Streetcars long ago disappeared in Seattle, but are making a comeback

Above: Seattle's first streetcar began running in 1884, a horse-drawn line up Second Avenue from Pioneer Square to Pike Street. Three years later, a cable-car line was established from Pioneer Square to Leschi Park, and in 1889 the city's first electric streetcars began running. Interurban service began in 1893, with the construction of a line to Geo 'getown. Work on a line to Renton began in 1889, and Ballard was reached in 1890. By 1898 there were over twenty independent streetcar lines in the area, most of which were consolidated into the Seattle Electric Company. This group began service to Tacoma in 1902 and Everett in 1910. Shown here around that year is an express car of the Seattle, Renton, and Southern's Rainier Valley Line. At that time, it was the only independently owned street railway in town, though the city would begin its own system in 1914.

Right: In 1919 the Seattle Municipal Railway absorbed the lines of the Seattle Electric Company, many of which had already been undergoing cutbacks due to the rise of the automobile. Interurban service slowed more in the 1920s, and shut down for good in 1939. That same year, the Seattle Municipal Railway became the Seattle Transit System, and switched to buses in 1941. Postwar sprawl brought calls for the return of a regional transit system, but it wasn't until 1973 that the countywide Municipality of Metropolitan Seattle, created in 1958 as a sewer agency, absorbed Seattle Transit. In 1990 they built a rail-ready bus tunnel under downtown Seattle. Proposals for new rail lines would come and go until 1996, when Sound Transit was created. Finally, in 2009, the Central Link light-rail system began operating in the tunnel, with service south to Sea-Tac Airport and extensions planned to North Seattle and the Eastside. Seen here is one of its trains heading down Martin Luther King Jr. Way South through the Rainier Valley.

HUSKY STADIUM

A much better name for a sporting venue than Sun Dodgers Stadium

Athletics at the University of Washington dates to at least 1889, when the school was still located on Denny's Knoll overlooking downtown Seattle. That Thanksgiving, the university football team played a group of Ivy League alumni, and were shut out, 20–0. In 1895 the school left downtown for a large wooded tract north of Portage Bay. Denny Field, in the northeast corner of campus, became the new athletic ground, and over the next few years both men's and women's basketball and rowing teams were formed. From 1908 to 1916, Washington's football coach was the legendary Gil Dobie, and during that time the team went undefeated. Their sixty-three-game unbeaten run, which ended in 1917, is still a college record. A 30,000-seat stadium, seen here in 1925, was built in 1920 next to Union Bay. It became known as Husky Stadium after 1922, the year Huskies was chosen over Malamutes as the athletic teams' mascot, replacing Sun Dodgers, a reference to the state's fickle climate.

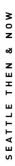

The Huskies have played over a hundred football games against their cross-state rivals, the Washington State Cougars. Known as the Apple Cup, the annual showdown caps the regular season, and is played at Husky Stadium every other year. Having undergone multiple renovations and the construction of two covered grandstands, the stadium is almost unrecognizable from the original design. It now seats 72,500 and, in addition to hosting football and track, is the site of the university's graduation ceremonies. The 1990 Goodwill Games were held here, as were two Seattle Seahawks seasons while Qwest Field was being built. Perhaps the most notable non-sports–related incident at Husky Stadium was the 1987 collapse of the north grandstand, which was then being built. A planned reconstruction of the ninety-year-old facility is due to begin once funding has been secured. This became necessary when the state balked at using sales-tax revenue.

FREMONT AVENUE

Enjoying fluctuating prosperity over the last hundred years

Left: White settlement in Fremont dates to the 1850s, but it wasn't until 1888 that development began in earnest. That year, Edward and Carrie Blewett, in association with Edward Corliss Kilbourne and Luther H. Griffith, plotted a 240-acre tract just north of Lake Union. Blewett and Griffith named the site after their hometown of Fremont, Nebraska. Also in 1888, widening began of Ross Creek, which separated Fremont from Queen Anne and was named after those mid-century settlers. In addition, Isaac Burlingame established a sawmill that year, and Kilbourne and Griffith, as well as Guy Phinney, soon began to build streetcar lines. The bridge shown here was built in 1892, a year after Fremont—already boasting a population of 5,000—was annexed to the city, and the approximate date of this photograph. A streetcar can be seen heading down Lake Avenue—soon to be renamed after the neighborhood—from Phinney's Woodland Park estate.

Above: Fremont maintained an industrial character for many years, and prospered with the arrival of interurban rail in 1910, the Northern Pacific Railway in 1914, and the Lake Washington Ship Canal and Fremont Bridge in 1917. However, the Pacific Highway bypassed it in 1932, and the cessation of passenger rail service in 1941 put Fremont into further decline. In the 1960s, members of the counterculture started to move in. Fremont began to revel in its quirkiness, billing itself as the "Center of the Universe." This reputation was cemented when a bust of Vladimir Lenin, salvaged from post-communist Slovakia, was erected near the neighborhood's heart. However, just as the statue was going up in 1995, Fremont's fortunes began to change, as dot-coms and their workers discovered the inexpensive neighborhood. Office parks have sprung up on the old mill sites, as has new construction on the main streets, though many of the buildings in this shot date from the early part of the last century.

KINGDOME SITE / QWEST FIELD

The Kingdome lasted less than a quarter of a century

Above: Professional sports in Seattle began on May 24, 1890, when the Seattle Base Ball Club beat a team from Spokane 11-8. By 1913 the city had a minor-league baseball team, the Giants, and a new stadium in the Rainier Valley, Dugdale Field. This stadium burned in 1932. In 1938 the new owner, Emil Sick of the Rainier Brewing Company, built a new stadium on the site. He named the team after his company, and the stadium after himself. For the next thirty years, the Rainiers called Sick's Stadium home. However, in 1969 the American League came to town in the form of the Seattle Pilots, and displaced the minor leaguers. The Pilots lasted one season before becoming the Milwaukee Brewers; the old stadium, which the city had promised to replace, took much of the blame. Finally, in 1972, a new site was chosen: the Burlington Northern rail yards south of Pioneer Square. The site is shown here in 1971, with the Seafirst Building (1969), Smith Tower (1914), and King Street Station (1906) visible in the distance.

Right: This decision was not without controversy, as the new site abutted two historic districts: Pioneer Square and Chinatown. The latter had also recently been cut in two by the construction of Interstate 5, and saw a series of protests. Finally, in March 1976, the King County Multipurpose Domed Stadium—the Kingdome—opened with a soccer match. The next year, pro baseball returned to Seattle and pro football made its first appearance, with the inaugural seasons of the Mariners and Seahawks. However, in the 1990s, the teams' new owners—Nintendo and Microsoft cofounder Paul Allen, respectively—began calling for new, dedicated, publicly funded stadiums as the price of staying in town. A leaky roof and partial ceiling collapse bolstered their arguments. After a failed vote and emergency legislative action, Safeco Field was built for the Mariners in 1999. The Kingdome, whose bonds had not yet been paid for, was demolished in 2000. Qwest Field, seen here looking up Occidental Avenue South, opened on the site in 2002.

LICTON SPRINGS

Briefly a spa; one of the city's only Native American place-names

In 1870 Seattle pioneers David and Arthur Denny bought 560 acres of land north of Green Lake. David's parcel included some of the only mineral springs in the area. These northern springs were well known to the Duwamish Indians, who called them *liq'tid*. Commonly translated as "red" or "painted," this referred to the orange mud produced by the iron springs' runoff that they used as face paint and a medicinal rub. David planned to build a spa, but this never came to fruition, and he died in 1903. After the city turned down the chance to buy the springs from his estate, they were sold to developers, and Licton Springs Park was plotted in 1909. Most of the land was built on, but just over seven acres, including the springs, were reserved as open space. The creek draining Licton Springs into Green Lake was covered in 1920, and connected to a storm drain in 1931. A spa was finally built in 1935 by Edward Jensen, and is seen here in 1945.

Jensen died in 1951, and the springs passed into the hands of A. R. Patterson, who planned a luxury resort for the grounds. However, in 1954 the city annexed all the land west of First Avenue Northeast as far north as 145th Street, and targeted the springs as a public park. This became reality in 1960. The spa was demolished, and in 1968 funds were made available for picnic and play areas. Construction finished in 1975; the equipment seen here dates from a 1987 renovation. Meanwhile, the city has grown up around Licton Springs, which, along with Shilshole Bay, is one of the only Native American place names still in use within the city. Aurora Avenue North, the former U.S. Highway 99, has been a major arterial for over eighty years, and Northgate Mall and North Seattle Community College were established east of the springs in 1950 and 1970, respectively.

WASHINGTON PARK ARBORETUM

Designed twice by the Olmsted brothers, the sons of Frederick Law Olmsted

Above: In 1900 the Puget Mill Company—established forty-eight years earlier in Port Gamble on the Olympic Peninsula—gave the city of Seattle sixty-two acres of a tract it owned along Union Bay. This was done in exchange for utility work on the land they held back for development. The subdivision, known as Broadmoor, opened in 1924 and consisted of a gated residential community surrounded by a horseshoe-shaped golf course. Meanwhile, the city began to expand Washington Park, as it had been named, acquiring land to the north, west, and south until it encompassed 260 acres. A boulevard was developed as part of the Olmsted brothers' 1903 parks and boulevard plan and in anticipation of the upcoming Alaska-Yukon-Pacific Exposition on the campus of the University of Washington. It is seen here in 1911 under a brick sewer trestle the city had built that year in the alignment of Lynn Street.

Right: The park's Azalea Way had become a favorite spot for harness racing and other equestrian activities, but this all came to an end in the 1930s, when the university finally realized its plans for a formal arboretum. These had dated to its move north in 1895, but as much of the campus underwent development, those in favor were forced to look across Union Bay to what was still native growth. Conversion began in the mid-1920s, and the Washington Park Arboretum was formally established under the management of the university in December 1934. The Olmsted brothers' firm also designed this incarnation of the park. It was their last of many commissions in Seattle, which had encompassed nearly every major park and boulevard. The arboretum, having mostly survived the threat of freeway construction in the 1960s, now operates as part of the university's botanic gardens, which contain nearly 4,400 plant species. The trestle was made a city landmark in 1976 and a federal landmark in 1982.

U.S. IMMIGRATION STATION AND ASSAY OFFICE

Sometimes known as Seattle's own Ellis Island

Pioneer settlers aside, the history of immigration in Seattle begins around 1860, when Chinese began to move north from San Francisco in search of work. They were followed by large numbers of Japanese and Filipinos. These communities largely settled in Chinatown and Japantown, southeast of downtown. Other large immigrant groups included Scandinavians, Italians, and Sephardic Jews. To cope with the influx, the federal government opened a new immigration station in 1932 on Airport Way South. Located just below Chinatown between Fifth and Sixth avenues, it was mere blocks from Union and King Street stations, and in close proximity to the steamer docks. It replaced not only the old immigration station at the foot of Union Street but also the assay office on First Hill that saw so much business during the Klondike gold rush. Known as "Seattle's Ellis Island," it is seen here shortly after its opening.

The immigration station, which was added to the National Register of Historic Places in 1979, also served as a detention center. Chinese immigrants with suspicious paperwork—legitimate or not—were frequent targets, as were Japanese Americans and other "enemy aliens" during World War II. As the years passed, the station became more and more of a detention center and office building due to an increase in illegal immigration and the ascendancy of air over rail and sea travel. A work-release center and federal prison were proposed for the site in the 1980s, but met fierce opposition from the neighborhood and local government. The building finally closed in 2004 after the immigration offices moved to Tukwila and Sea-Tac Airport and a new detention center was built in Tacoma. It currently serves as a homeless shelter while awaiting redevelopment.

WASHINGTON HIGH SCHOOL / SEATTLE CENTRAL COMMUNITY COLLEGE

From premier h gh school to top community college

This photo shows Washington High School on graduation day in 1908. The stone edifice at the corner of Broadway and Pine Street was erected in 1902 at a cost of $250,000. The city's first purpose-built high school, it was originally named Seattle High. It was designed by William E. Boone and James M. Corner. At the time of this commission, Boone was already seventy-two years old, but had been very active during the 1880s. Many of his structures were burned in the Great Fire of 1889. In 1906 Seattle High took its new name in anticipation of the 1907 opening of the district's second high school, Lincoln, in Wallingford. There had originally been concern over Washington High's size—it had room for nearly double the number of Seattle's high-school students when it was built—but a growing population and the 1907 addition of night classes for adults meant the school had to expand into a number of annexes.

In October 1908, Washington High was renamed Broadway after the arterial on which it stood. In 1911 an addition designed by Edgar Blair was erected at the corner of Pine and Harvard Avenue; this building still stands as the Broadway Performance Hall. Broadway High continued to grow, and had an enrollment nearing 2,400 by 1936. However, demographic changes during World War II—not the least of which was the Japanese internment, which affected a quarter of the school's students—reduced enrollment to 1,200 in 1944. Broadway High closed in 1946, and its buildings and vocational and evening schools became part of the new Broadway-Edison Technical School, which also catered to returning veterans. This became Seattle Community College in 1966, which was renamed Seattle Central Community College in 1970 with the opening of additional campuses in the north and south of the city. Seattle Central has educated nearly half a million students since its founding, and currently has an enrollment of 10,000, a third of whom hail from other nations.

MOORE THEATRE

One of the country's most lavishly appointed theaters when it opened

Left: Seen here in 1909 is the Moore Theatre, located at the southeast corner of Second Avenue and Virginia Street. The nearly 2,400-seat theater was built in 1907 by James A. Moore, who was a major developer of Green Lake, West Seattle, and Capitol Hill, giving the latter its name as well as its subdivisions. It was billed as the third-largest in the country, and was certainly the largest in the state. Designed by noted theater architect E. W. Houghton, the construction cost $350,000. John Cort, one of the founders of the Fraternal Order of Eagles, was the original lessee, and ran the Moore for its first few seasons. To its south stood the New Washington Hotel. The grand Denny Hotel stood on this spot before the neighborhood was leveled.

Above: The Moore is the oldest theater in town, having survived the end of vaudeville, changing popular tastes, and a brief stint in the 1970s as a repertory film house called the Moore Egyptian. In this latter guise, it was the inaugural venue of the Seattle International Film Festival. Renovations, though reducing its capacity, have increased its comfort, and today the Moore hosts everything from musical concerts and dramatic performances to literary readings and live radio. It became a federal landmark in 1974 and a city one in 1989. The neighboring hotel, now known as the Josephinum, became a city landmark the same year. It now serves as low-income housing and is the headquarters of the Archdiocesan Housing Authority of Catholic Community Services.

FREDERICK AND NELSON / NORDSTROM BUILDING

Flagship store of two iconic Seattle retailers

Left: In 1890, Colorado miners Donald E. Frederick and James Mecham founded a used-furniture store in downtown Seattle. Soon thereafter, a Swedish immigrant by the name of Nels B. Nelson took Mecham's place in the firm, and it became known as Frederick and Nelson. They soon began selling new goods and rapidly established a reputation for excellent customer service. As Seattle's population grew during the gold rush years, so too did the department store's business. In 1918, eleven years after Nelson's death, Frederick opened this new building at the corner of Fifth Avenue and Pine Street. He sold the store in 1929 to Chicago's Marshall Field and Company. It is shown here in 1945, with the 1925 Medical Dental Building to its north. Meanwhile, another Swedish immigrant, John W. Nordstrom, had founded a shoe store in 1901 with Carl F. Wallin. By 1945 there were two Nordstrom locations: one in the University District, and the flagship just a block south of Frederick and Nelson.

Above: "Freddie's" had expanded to fifteen stores by the end of the 1970s, but its fortunes soon began to change. BATUS Inc. bought Marshall Field's in 1980, and sold off the Seattle division to locals six years later. Frederick and Nelson changed hands once again in 1989, but declared bankruptcy in 1991 and closed the next year. Nordstrom's fortunes, however, were quite the opposite. Exclusively a shoe store since its founding, it began selling apparel in 1963. Over the next three decades, Nordstrom embarked on a nationwide expansion. When the Frederick and Nelson Building—to which had been added five extra stories in 1952—fell vacant, Nordstrom bought it. The building became a city landmark in 1997, and opened as Nordstrom's new flagship store in 1998. Nordstrom remains one of the country's premier department stores, and recently opened its first store in Manhattan.

MADISON PARK

A new beach was created when the lake dropped by nine feet

Left: John J. McGilvra began his law practice in 1853 in an Illinois office adjacent to that of Abraham Lincoln. They became friends, and in 1861 Lincoln appointed McGilvra U.S. attorney for the Washington Territory. McGilvra moved to Seattle in 1864. That year, he purchased 420 acres on the shore of Lake Washington just south of Union Bay; the land was being sold by the government to finance the Territorial University of Washington. In 1865 McGilvra cut Madison Street through from downtown Seattle, the only road to cross the entire city without interruption. After a brief term as city attorney, McGilvra began to subdivide his Laurel Shade estate in the 1880s. To entice the public, he founded the Madison Street Cable Railway Company and dedicated a lakefront park at its terminus, with service beginning in 1891. There was also ferry service across Lake Washington to Kirkland. This photo of the concessions area was likely taken in 1910, the very year streetcar service was cut back to Capitol Hill.

Above: The shoreline in this modern view is literally a different one from that in the 1910 photograph, as the level of Lake Washington dropped nine feet in 1916 during the construction of the Ship Canal to Lake Union and Puget Sound. This newly exposed land became a city park along with the old parcel in 1922. Its southern portion was developed into a bathing beach, which today draws swimmers from the entire city; the northern portion, seen here, was left in a tree-filled, rocky state for passive recreation. Visible in the distance are a fishing pier, located where the Kirkland ferry once docked, as well as the west high-rise of the Evergreen Point Floating Bridge. The ferry's last run was in 1950, having been made redundant by the opening of the Lake Washington Floating Bridge to Mercer Island in 1940.

MADISON PARK FERRY

Made redundant by the Lake Washington Floating Bridge

By the time this undated picture was taken—sometime in the 1930s or early 1940s—pioneer John J. McGilvra's Laurel Shade estate had long since developed into the bustling neighborhood of Madison Park. This was helped in no small part by a cable car running from downtown to the ferry dock at the foot of East Madison Street on Lake Washington. Though the eastern half of the streetcar's route was discontinued in 1910, ferries kept making the cross-lake run to the shipyards and wool mills of Kirkland. The Lake Washington Floating Bridge, which opened in 1940, connected Seattle's Mount Baker neighborhood to Mercer Island, and thence to Bellevue. It took away some business, but the advent of war the next year brought much activity to the Lake Washington Shipyard, keeping the ferry running profitably for a few more years.

Ridership dropped as the floating bridge became more popular, and the ferry's last run was on August 31, 1950. When a second bridge was built from Seattle to Medina in 1963, it bypassed Madison Park completely. The neighborhood settled into its current affluent character, filled with boutiques, restaurants, pubs, and a bathing beach that draws swimmers from the entire city. The 1921 building to the north of the terminal still survives, though the terminal itself does not; the approach to the lake is lined with condominiums, and the ferry dock is now a small fishing pier. The city park is just visible to the south, and the 1963 bridge is in the distance. Kirkland and the rest of the Eastside lie beyond, having escaped the proposed construction of a third cross-lake bridge in the 1960s. Some have suggested the resurrection of ferry service in lieu of a rebuilt bridge—the Evergreen Point Floating Bridge is at risk of collapsing during an earthquake—but this part of East Madison Street is likely to remain quiet for the foreseeable future.

INDIAN CAMP AND STATE WAMPI.

BALLAST ISLAND

The Duwamish tribe, now 600 strong, once again owns land

Left: Seattle's indigenous residents are the Duwamish tribe of Native Americans. It is not known when their ancestors arrived on the shores of Whulge—a Lushootseed name, meaning "salt water," for Puget Sound—but archaeological evidence points to no later than 4,000 years ago, and likely closer to 9,000. Before the arrival of Europeans, they were the Dkhw'Duw'Absh and Xachua'bsh, meaning "People Inside the Bay" and "People of the Large Lake"; the combined tribe became known in English as the Duwamish. The first white settlers reached Seattle in 1851; a mere four years later, the Treaty of Point Elliott was signed, consigning the Duwamish and other area tribes to reservations and dispersing their local settlements. Shown here in the early 1890s—around the same time the last permanent Duwamish camp is said to have been destroyed—is a temporary settlers' camp on the artificial Ballast Island off Pioneer Square, often used as a stop on their way to and from the hop fields.

Above: Ballast Island was soon buried under Railroad Avenue; today, at the foot of Washington Street stands a 1920 boat landing that once housed Seattle's harbormaster. Settlers were quick to honor Duwamish chief Si'ahl by naming their new town after him and their river after his tribe, yet the Duwamish people struggled for recognition throughout the twentieth century. They never received their own reservation, and were only briefly federally recognized in 2001 before this decision was reversed. The Duwamish have always maintained a tribal organization, however, and in 1983 formally created Duwamish Tribal Services under the leadership of Cecile Hansen, a descendant of Chief Si'ahl's family. In 2009 the nearly 600-member tribe opened the Duwamish Longhouse and Cultural Center on the west bank of the Duwamish River (inset), near the site of one of their old settlements. This was their first longhouse, and first independently owned property, in over 150 years.

FORTY-FIFTH STREET THEATRE

Bucking the trend of home entertainment and multiplexes

This photo shows William Bruen's Forty-fifth Street Theatre as it looked one night—bargain night, apparently—in 1934. A twin bill of Barbara Stanwyck's *Ever in My Heart* and the early science-fiction movie *Deluge* appear on the marquee. Founded in 1921 as the Paramount, the theater was designed by George Purvis, who was also responsible for movie houses in Longview, Olympia, and Port Angeles. In 1933 the Paramount was bought by Bruen and given his name, as well as an Art Moderne facelift. At the time, it was one of many independent movie houses in Seattle, including the Majestic, Egyptian, Fox, Coliseum, Portola, Broadway, Uptown, and Neptune. Built in an advantageous location along the Wallingford neighborhood's main commercial street, it seated 500, and was often filled.

In 1955 Bob Clark bought the Forty-fifth Street Theatre, added "Guild" to its name, and turned it into an art house. Twenty-eight years later, a subsequent owner by the name of Randy Finley opened a sister theater just down the street. The Guild II had essentially the same name, so the two houses came to be differentiated by their paint jobs: the original was the "pink theater," the new one the "blue." The national chain Landmark Theatres bought Finley's group of Seven Gables Theatres in 1989. By that time, it included most of Seattle's remaining art houses, including the Neptune. Despite the dominance of blockbusters, multiplexes, DVDs, and the Internet in the years since, the theater's two screens do brisk business to this day. It stands as one of the oldest continually operating movie theaters in the city.

LESCHI PARK

The last of Seattle's cable car lines ran through Leschi Park

J. M. Thompson and Fred Sander's Yesler Way cable car was the first in Seattle to run from Elliott Bay to Lake Washington, making its first run in the fall of 1887. This spurred the development of a park near the old sawmills. Leschi Park, which was part of the Olmsted brothers' plan for Seattle's parks and boulevards in 1903, included Seattle's first zoo, which moved to Woodland Park that same year. Around 1900 the cable line was bought out of bankruptcy by the Seattle Electric Company, a private concern then consolidating its streetcar ownership. In 1909 this entity built the iron pergola in Pioneer Square as its western terminal. This photo was taken the next year from the top of the viaduct carrying the line over the deep ravine to the waterfront. Near the powerhouse was a ferry dock providing service to Bellevue and Medina. The neighborhood, once a Duwamish settlement, was named for the Nisqually chief Leschi, who took part in the 1856 Battle of Seattle and was hanged two years later.

The city took over the Yesler line in 1919, forming the Seattle Municipal Railway. Soon thereafter, the ferry system was acquired by King County. The cable car—the city's last—kept running until August 1940, when it was replaced by a bus line. With the opening of the Lake Washington Floating Bridge the same year from Mount Baker to Mercer Island, cross-lake ferry service became redundant. A marina now stands at the foot of the Yesler right-of-way across Lakeside Avenue from the park, and a few offices, restaurants, and small stores line the street to the north, but otherwise the lakefront is occupied by housing and public beaches. Lake Washington Boulevard, which parallels the shore from Denny-Blaine to Seward Park, makes an inland detour here. It can be seen at left heading under this remnant of the viaduct, which is now indistinguishable from the parkland below.

MARKET STREET

Still Ballard's main drag

Left: While an independent city from 1890 to 1907, Ballard's commercial core was located along Ballard Avenue. Upon annexation, however, development shifted north to Market Street. This photo shows the north side of Market, just east of Twenty-second Avenue, in October 1925. Situated one block north of the former city hall, the block included the Ballard Court Apartments, owned by the Pheasant-Wiggen Mortuary, which operated out of the ground floor. On the other side of Ballard Hall, a commercial building, stands the Majestic Theatre, built in 1915, which offered silent movies and vaudeville performances. At the far right is Ballard's Carnegie Free Public Library, built in 1904 with $15,000 donated by Andrew Carnegie, who had also pledged $200,000 toward a new central library for Seattle. Its architect, Henderson Ryan, also designed the Neptune Theatre in the University District.

Above: Northwest Market Street remains Ballard's main commercial thoroughfare, though Ballard Avenue is still the neighborhood's cultural heart. Despite massive construction efforts in the last two decades, many of Ballard's historic buildings remain standing, if not fulfilling their original functions. The mortuary building, for a while home to a Sears, Roebuck store, is now a café in the local Tully's chain. The library, replaced by a new building in 1963, was added to the National Register of Historic Places in 1979, and is now home to a French restaurant and private offices. The Majestic, which was renamed the Roxy in 1929 and the Bay in 1948, was reputedly the oldest movie theater west of the Mississippi, but fell into disrepair and closed in the late 1990s. In 2000 a new theater, the Majestic Bay, rose on the site. It remains one of the few independent movie houses in the city.

BALLARD CITY HALL / MARVIN'S GARDEN

Once an independent city, now an urban village

Left: This photograph shows the Ballard substation of the Seattle Police Department in 1915. A mere eight years earlier, it was the city hall of an independent Ballard—the second-largest town in King County. Ballard was homesteaded in 1852, but remained forested and undeveloped for many years. In the 1880s, much of it came into the hands of the West Coast Improvement Company, owned by Judge Thomas Burke, Daniel H. Gilman, and John Leary. William Rankin Ballard won an adjacent tract in a coin toss. Soon thereafter, lumber and shingle mills began to spring up on the shores of Salmon and Shilshole bays. Incorporated in 1889, by 1900 Ballard was Washington's seventh-largest city, billing itself as the "Shingle Capital of the World." It became the center of Scandinavian settlement in the region, and by 1907 its population had more than tripled again. However, the young city found itself unable to cope with its rapid growth, and annexed itself to Seattle on May 29 of that year.

Above: Today, this site is occupied by Marvin's Garden, named for the late unofficial mayor of the neighborhood, Marvin Sjoberg. The Ballard Centennial Bell Tower, dedicated in 1989, stands at the corner of Twenty-second and Ballard avenues, and houses the original half-ton brass bell, most famously rung in mourning to announce Ballard's annexation. The old city hall itself was demolished in 1965. Plaques commemorate the creation in 1976 of the federal Ballard Avenue Historical District, designated by joint proclamation of Seattle's mayor and the king of Sweden. An industrial district still exists along Salmon Bay, though it has been encroached upon by commercial development. Designated an "urban village" in the 1990s, Ballard has seen its density increase with the construction of numerous condominium and retail projects; this has resulted in the dilution of its Scandinavian character, though it remains home to the Nordic Heritage Museum.